TWAYNE'S WORLD AUTHORS SERIES

A Survey of the World's Literature

Sylvia E. Bowman, Indiana University

GENERAL EDITOR

FRANCE

Maxwell A. Smith, Guerry Professor of French, Emeritus
The University of Chattanooga
Former Visiting Professor in Modern Languages
The Florida State University

EDITOR

Benjamin Constant

(TWAS 297)

TWAYNE'S WORLD AUTHORS SERIES (TWAS)

The purpose of TWAS is to survey the major writers —novelists, dramatists, historians, poets, philosophers, and critics—of the nations of the world. Among the national literatures covered are those of Australia, Canada, China, Eastern Europe, France, Germany, Greece, India, Italy, Japan, Latin America, the Netherlands, New Zealand, Poland, Russia, Scandinavia, Spain, and the African nations, as well as Hebrew, Yiddish, and Latin Classical literatures. This survey is complemented by Twayne's United States Authors Series and English Authors Series.

The intent of each volume in these series is to present a critical-analytical study of the works of the writer; to include biographical and historical material that may be necessary for understanding, appreciation, and critical appraisal of the writer; and to present all material in clear, concise English—but not to vitiate the scholarly content of the work by doing so.

Benjamin Constant

By JOHN CRUICKSHANK
University of Sussex — England

Twayne Publishers, Inc.   ::   New York

Library of Congress Cataloging in Publication Data

Cruickshank, John.
  Benjamin Constant.

  (Twayne's world authors series, TWAS 297. France)
  Bibliography: p.
  1. Constant de Rebecque, Henri Benjamin, 1767–1830—
Criticism and interpretation.
PQ2211.C24C7 848′.6′09   73–21952
ISBN 0–8057–2242–4

ISBN 0–8057–2242–4

Preface

This volume does not claim to be a piece of original research. In the main it relies on the pioneering work of the many brilliant scholars, from Rudler onwards, who have contributed to Constant studies. Naturally, the interpretation of their conclusions is my own and breaks some new ground. However, my chief purpose has been to provide a general, readable, and up-to-date study not only of Constant's fictional works, but also of his main writings on politics and religion.

Undergraduate courses tend to present Constant almost exclusively as the author of *Adolphe*. It is customary to see him chiefly as an interesting, rather isolated figure in the history of the French novel as it developed at the beginning of the nineteenth century. As a result, students rarely read more than *Adolphe* itself, and possibly *Cécile* (a novel first published in 1951), or the autobiographical *Cahier rouge*. This is to do less than justice to the range and variety of Constant's talents and achievements. It is also to see his fiction in too narrow a focus.

With these considerations in mind, I have devoted a good deal of space to his political and religious writings as well as to his theoretical essays on literature, and quoted liberally from them. As a result, both the student of Constant and the general reader will be able to view and evaluate, in a more comprehensive way, his wide-ranging intellectual activity. If they are thereby tempted to read more widely beyond his novels and autobiographical writings, so much the better. Much of what he had to say retains its interest and fascination well over 150 years after it was written.

JOHN CRUICKSHANK

University of Sussex
Brighton, England

93040

Acknowledgment

I wish to record my gratitude to the Trustees of the Leverhulme Research Awards. Their generosity made it possible for me to complete the writing of this book in the fall of 1972.

Contents

Contents

Chronology

1767   Oct. 25: Benjamin Henri Constant de Rebecque born in Lausanne, son of Louis-Arnold-Juste Constant de Rebecque and Henriette-Pauline de Chandieu. Nov. 10: Mother dies.

1767– Family quarrels over his upbringing. Father finally hands
1772   Benjamin over to Marianne Mangin to whom he also gives a written undertaking of marriage, July 22, 1772.

1772– Series of unsatisfactory private tutors: Stroelin, De la
1781   Grange, Gobert, Duplessis. Travels with father, a lieutenant-colonel in the service of the Netherlands, to Belgium, Holland and England (London and Oxford). Writes incomplete *Les Chevaliers* described as a *roman héroïque en cinq chants*, 1778–79.

1782   Student at University of Erlangen from February till May of following year.

1783– Student at University of Edinburgh from July, 1783, till
1785   May, 1785. Takes part in debates of Speculative Society, voting in favor of execution of Charles I, higher education for women, etc. Friendships with Mackintosh, Wilde, Laing, and others. Growth of lifelong taste for gambling.

1785   Lodges in Paris with Suard family. First of numerous love affairs: with Mme Johannot in Brussels. In love with Mrs. Trevor in Lausanne toward end of year. Begins work on study of polytheism.

1787   First meeting and close friendship with Mme de Charrière. Jenny Pourrat affair. Sudden departure for England and Scotland in June, leaving with "three shirts, a few pairs of stockings and thirty-one louis," and returning (September) with syphilis.

1788   Duel at Colombier (home of Mme de Charrière near Neuchâtel) with Duplessis d'Épendes.

1788– Takes up position in court of Duke of Brunswick. Marries
1794   Wilhelmina von Cramm, 1789. Travels in Holland and

Switzerland. Reconciliation with Mme de Charrière, 1790. Break with Minna von Cramm, 1791. Liaison with Charlotte von Hardenberg, 1793.

1794 Sept. 18: First meeting with Mme de Staël. Falls madly in love.

1795 Resigns from Brunswick post. Attempted suicide. Arrives in Paris with Mme de Staël. Officially divorced from Minna.

1796 Printing in Switzerland of *De la force du gouvernement actuel de la France et de la nécessité de s'y rallier*. Challenges journalist Bertin de Veaux to duel.

1797 Publishes *Des réactions politiques* and *Des effects de la Terreur*. Founder member and secretary of the Club de Salm where he defends the Coup d'état. Birth of Albertine de Staël, probably Constant's daughter.

1798 Obtains French citizenship. Fails to be elected for Seine-et-Oise. Duel with journalist Sibuet. Friendship with Mme Julie Talma. Publishes *Des suites de la contre-révolution de 1660 en Angleterre*.

1799 Becomes a member of the Tribunat. Leading member of liberal opposition until his elimination in 1802.

1800 Love affair with Mme Lindsay until May 31 of following year.

1802 Death of Baron de Staël.

1803 Keeps his first-known private journal entitled *Amélie et Germaine*. Mme de Staël ordered to leave France on political grounds and Constant accompanies her to Germany.

1804 Meetings with Goethe, Schiller, and Wieland in Weimar. Continuing scenes with Mme de Staël who refuses to marry him. Renewal of affair with Charlotte von Hardenberg.

1805 Deaths of Mme Talma and Mme de Charrière. New passion for Anna Lindsay.

1806 Further meetings with Charlotte von Hardenberg. Working on novel *qui sera notre histoire* and of which the Ellénore episode later grew into *Adolphe*.

1807 Further scenes with Mme de Staël. Contacts with quietist sect in Lausanne. With Charlotte who is seriously ill in Besançon.

1808 Secret marriage to Charlotte. Joins Mme de Staël at Coppet.

1809 Publishes *Wallstein, tragédie en cinq actes et en vers, pré-*

cédéé de quelques réflexions sur le théâtre allemand. Continuing oscillation between Charlotte and Mme de Staël, who learns of his marriage.

1810 Sorting out financial obligations to Mme de Staël. Large gaming losses.

1811 Final break with Mme de Staël after 17 years. Probably begins to write *Cécile.* In Göttingen with Charlotte and working on *De la religion.*

1812 Quarrels with Charlotte. Death of his father.

1813 Contacts with Prince Bernadotte continue into following year.

1814 Publishes anti-Napoleonic *De l'esprit de conquête et de l'usurpation dans leurs rapports avec la civilisation européenne.* Also publishes *Réflexions sur les constitutions, la distribution des pouvoirs et les garanties dans une monarchie constitutionnelle, De la liberté des brochures, des pamphlets et des journaux* and *Observations sur le discours de S. E. le ministre de l'intérieur en faveur du projet de loi sur la liberté de la presse.* Passion for Mme Récamier. Readings from *Adolphe* in various salons.

1815 Duel with Montlosier. Maintains hostility toward Napoleon, takes brief refuge in U.S. Embassy in Paris, but has several interviews with Emperor during April and becomes *conseiller d'état.* Publication in May of *Principes de politique applicables à tous les gouvernements représentatifs.* June 20: Learns of Waterloo defeat and writes *apologia* for his actions during the Hundred Days. Order for his exile revoked by Louis XVIII. Religious influence of Mme de Krüdener.

1816 In England with Charlotte. Publication of *Adolphe* in London and Paris. Also publishes *De la doctrine qui peut réunir les partis en France* which is well received.

1817 Defends the *Charte* in series of articles in the *Mercure de France* and, after its suppression, in *La Minerve française.* Fails to be elected to Académie Française. Death of Mme de Staël.

1818 Publishes *Collection complète des ouvrages publiés sur le Gouvernement représentatif et la constitution actuelle de la France, formant une espèce de Cours de politique constitutionnelle* (4 vols.), 1818–20. Permanent limp as result of fall.

1819   Elected deputy for the Sarthe region.

1820   Publishes Part I of the *Mémoires sur les Cent-Jours.* Part II published 1822. Plays important role in debates following assassination of Duc de Berry. Speech on freedom of the press. Antagonistic reception in Saumur.

1821   Speaks against the slave trade.

1822   Duel (seated) with Forbin. Fails to be reelected as deputy for the Sarthe. Implication in Berton affair. Publishes *Commentaire sur l'ouvrage de Filangieri,* 1822–24.

1824   Elected deputy for Paris. Publishes first of five volumes constituting *De la religion considérée dans sa source, ses formes et ses développements.* Vol. II published in 1825, Vol. III in 1827, and Vols. IV and V posthumously in 1831. Third edition of *Adolphe.*

1825   Speech on law to indemnify the émigrés. Publishes *Appel aux nations chrétiennes en faveur des Grecs.*

1827   Reelected in Paris and elected in Strasbourg. Decides to represent latter as deputy for the Lower Rhine.

1828   Again fails to be elected to the Académie Française.

1829   Publishes *Mélanges de littérature et de politique* and contributes "Réflexions sur la tragédie" to the *Revue de Paris* in October. Severe deterioration in health.

1830   Reelected to the Chambre des députés in June. Increasing illness. Draws up declaration, with Sébastiani, in favor of Louis-Philippe. Becomes *conseiller d'état* again. Final failure to be elected to Académie Française. Dec. 8: Dies and is buried December 12 in Père-Lachaise cemetery after national funeral.

CHAPTER 1

Conflicts and Principles

BENJAMIN Constant was one of the most gifted men of his age—an age which included Goethe and Chateaubriand, Hegel and Maine de Biran, Napoleon and Talleyrand, Bentham and Malthus, Beethoven, Constable, and Coleridge. He did not possess the concentrated and single-minded genius of most of these contemporaries, but he surpassed them all, with the possible exception of Goethe, in the range and variety of his talents. He was a major liberal politician, the author of an outstanding novel, a leading parliamentary orator, a scholar whose lifelong work was an historical analysis of religion from fetishism to monotheism, a literary critic, a fascinating diarist, a distinguished political journalist, a cosmopolitan intellectual, a brilliant and witty social figure, a man whose love affairs brought him a European reputation. His many achievements and his immense public prestige were reflected in the state funeral which preceded his burial in the Père-Lachaise cemetery in Paris on 12 December 1830.

I Egoism and Dualism

Human beings are self-absorbed and inconsistent in much that they do. Constant was no exception. He possessed these characteristics to a notable degree and was fully aware of their central role in his makeup. There was a striking gap between his private shortcomings and his public successes, between his natural temperament and his social *persona*. Much of his life was restless and unhappy, given over to continual vacillation, self-analysis, and what Pascal termed "the internal warfare of man." The family motto was a play on words—*In arduis constans* —and many were inclined to take the game a stage further. In certain social circles in his native Lausanne, Constant was known as "Benjamin l'inconstant." His mocking self-awareness and intense preoccupation with his own character caused Constant himself, even more than his friends, to refer to this fact of his changing and divided personality. A typical statement is contained in the entry in his *Journal* for 11 April 1804 when he writes: ". . . I am not a completely real person. There are within me two people, one of whom is the observer of the other." [1] Earlier, in a letter to Mme de Charrière dated 6 July 1792, he had described himself as being "neither credulous nor incredulous, neither moral nor immoral."

In fact, he was each of these things in different ways and at different times. Indeed, it is possible to draw up a considerable list of contrasts which made up his complex character. He was both emotional and cerebral, timid and vain, generous and selfish, severely self-analytical and notably self-indulgent. He was a rationalist who possessed a sense of mystery, a believer in the possibility of human progress though a fundamental pessimist, a champion of political liberty who argued that individual character is irremediably determined. His self-indulgence did not prevent him from showing genuine concern for victims of injustice. In his relations with others he displayed both wounding frankness and an understanding sensitivity. He lacked willpower yet showed immense intellectual energy; the incoherence of his personal life was accompanied by considerable mental discipline. Above all, perhaps, he had a deep physical and emotional need of love—"I cannot do without women; they bring me genuine benefit and to be deprived of them upsets all my physical and moral faculties" [2]—yet he also had a thoroughgoing horror of dependence, of being bound to another human being by intimate ties and responsibilities. Indeed, this is the central dilemma analyzed in his brilliant and largely autobiographical novel, *Adolphe*. It is finally typical of Constant, however, that the entry in his *Journal* just quoted should have been followed a year later by one which reads: "I should much prefer study and solitude to all the women and all the love affairs in the world." [3]

We sometimes assume too readily that we ourselves lead thoroughly consistent lives. By the same token, we often demand an unreasonable degree of consistency in others. The fact of contradiction and dualism in human beings has been emphasized by moralists and psychologists from St. Paul to Freud, and it is clear that inner contrasts can be enriching as well as enfeebling. Quite apart from the confirmation of his humanity to be found in Constant's protean nature, his response to his own dualism was, in several ways, a source of strength. Most notably, his inner tensions released the creative energy that went into the making of *Adolphe* and such autobiographical writings as *Le Cahier rouge* (*The Red Notebook*) and the *Journaux intimes* (*Private Journals*). It could also be argued that private disorders strengthened his consistent stand on a number of public issues. His need for moral order and intellectual coherence was projected outwards. Not least of all, Constant's divided nature encouraged in him a sense of complexity, an avoidance of simple, unilinear solutions, the ability to see several aspects of a problem. In 1794, writing to Mme de Charrière, he notes "this strange mania which enables me to see the opposite sides of a thing one after the other." [4] It is true that he describes himself as being "tired" of this particular "mania," but he was fairer to himself ten years later when he wrote to his aunt, Mme de Nassau: "Why, pray, should I be accused of weakness of character? This is an accusation to which all *enlightened* people are exposed because they see the two, or rather the thousand, aspects of things. Because they are unable to reach a decision they appear to waver, now in one direction, now in another." [5]

Constant is grappling here with the eternal problem of the genuine intellectual—the ability to see shades of color and the inability to pronounce in terms of black or white. Inevitably, he has been accused of hesitation and procrastination—and characteristically he is his own foremost accuser in the *Journal*. Much of his indecision, in fact, is more emotional than intellectual. It is noticeable above all in his love affairs and is of the kind which he fictionalized in *Adolphe* and *Cécile* or experienced at first hand in his relations with Mme de Staël, Charlotte von Hardenberg, and Mme Récamier. Furthermore, even on this point Constant was two-sided. He could also be impulsive in his love affairs as indeed he proved impulsive, on occasion, in the spheres of politics and religion. Intellectual caution and and emotional spontaneity were both present in his behavior as politician, lover, and religious thinker. And both were used, in different ways, to serve a number of principles to which he clung steadfastly while living with his own tensions and moods.

Among these principles may be noted, at this stage, his defense of individual freedom, his opposition to bigotry and oppression, his detestation of violence. He cherished these principles in politics, love, and religion and it is in these latter areas of major human concern, and also in literature, that he displayed his many-sided character most notably and achieved lasting distinction.

II *Freedom*

Constant's views on political liberty and individual freedom were forthright. He regarded both these forms of freedom as being closely related and was proud to have served them both:

For forty years I have defended the same principle—freedom in all things—in religion, in philosophy, in literature, in industry and in politics. By freedom I mean the triumph of individualsm as much over authority which seeks to govern by despotic means as over the masses which claim the right to enslave the minority to the majority. Despotism has no rights. The majority has the right to oblige the minority to respect public order, but everything which does not disturb public order, everything which is purely personal such as our opinions, everything which, in giving expression to opinions, does no harm to others either by provoking physical violence or opposing contrary opinions, everything which, in industry, allows a rival industry to flourish freely —all this is something individual that cannot legitimately be surrendered to the power of the state.[6]

This passage, from Constant's preface to his *Mélanges de littérature et de politique* (*Miscellany of Literary and Political Writings*), 1829, makes it clear that he identified freedom in part with economic liberalism and the doctrine of "laissez-faire." He lacked Sismondi's insight into the potentially unjust social consequences of free competition. Something will be said of this in a later chapter, but for the moment we are concerned with the origins of his conception of freedom rather than its implications.

It is not surprising that J.-J. Coulmann, in his *Notice sur Benjamin Constant* published in 1831, spoke of Constant's instinctive love of liberty and claimed that he worshiped freedom with the same intensity that other men have displayed in the worship of power. The impulse behind this concern with freedom is to be found in Constant's idea of personal autonomy and of an area within individual consciousness which must be wholly private, and in this sense free. It is a freedom predicated on the everpresent possibility of a conflict of interests between the self and everything else outside it. Personal conviction and private conscience must be preserved inviolate from all interference. This is no doubt a natural attitude in a person as self-absorbed as Constant. He inevitably fought for freedom on the frontier separating individualism from collectivism. At the same time, he was thoroughly aware of the fact that the individual, whose freedom is so important, is in a certain sense fettered and imprisoned by internal contradictions and conflicting impulses. He insisted, however, that human dualism must be seen and solved in *moral* terms only, and he specifically rejected Rousseau's *social* explanation, and collectivist political solution, of the fact of human alienation.

In the seventeenth century the internal conflicts which men experience were still interpreted in moral or religious terms. In his *Pensées*, for example, Pascal saw man as a "dispossessed monarch" in exile from a kingdom of moral perfection over which he had once ruled. Pascal argued that the inner warfare which man experiences, a contest between desired perfection and inevitably imperfect achievement, is due to the fact of original sin which caused man to fall from that original state of self-coincidence for which he was created by God and of which he still retains vestigial memories. In the eighteenth century, and particularly in the writings of Rousseau, a social theory replaced earlier moral and religious interpretations. Rousseau agreed, in his *Discours sur l'inégalité parmi les hommes*, that man was originally endowed with natural goodness, but he located the subsequent principle of corruption in forms of social organization, not original sin. At the same time Rousseau believed that man could only become a unified moral being by living in society. It was impossible, and indeed undesirable, to put the clock back to "presocietal" man and consequently society needed to be altered drastically in a way that would alone enable the individual to overcome his "alienation." In a word, social surgery must replace divine grace as the means of liberating man from the constraints and conflicts of self-division. In Rousseau's system this involved the individual's finding freedom not in pure personal autonomy, but in assent to the "general will"—the synthesis of individual wills in a true community representing the better nature of each and expressed in the decisions and laws of the state.

In his *Principes de politique* published in 1815, Constant agrees with Rousseau that the "general will" or "sovereignty of the people" must be regarded as the only basis of legitimate political authority. He vigorously denies, however, that such authority possesses absolute power over the individual. He maintains that "there is, on the contrary, a part of human existence which, of necessity, remains individual and independent, being legitimately placed outside all social jurisdiction." [7] This is a fundamental point which marks Constant's total rejection of all revolutionary doctrines that ultimately derive their theories from the sentimental abstractions of Rousseau and claim that the basic dilemmas of man, his alienation from himself and from others, can be satisfactorily solved in social and political terms. What Rousseau had done was to conflate individual freedom and political liberty whereas Constant insisted on distinguishing between them. Rather than seeking to strengthen the state against anarchical individualism, Constant was primarily concerned to preserve the freedom of human beings from state oppression, ideological control, and bureaucratic interference. He interpreted the ideas set out in Rousseau's *Contrat social* as offering "pretexts for all forms of tyranny" [8] and gave as an example the situation which existed under the Terror of 1793–94 when private freedom was crushed by violent and murderous means as a result of ideas originally popularized by such political theorists as Mably and Rousseau himself. "The sovereignty of the people," in fact, became an excuse used by tyrants to destroy their opponents, muzzle free expression, and impose their will.

Apart from the practical evils which resulted from the identification of personal freedom with a certain conception of political liberty, Constant believed that much revolutionary theory was mistaken on a different level. In *De l'esprit de conquête et de l'usurpation* of 1814, he maintained that the men of 1789 made the major error of applying, quite inappropriately, the political and social ideas of the Greek *polis* to modern times. He argued that the concept of civil liberty as we know it was virtually nonexistent among the Ancients. They operated in terms of a collective liberty which we would find an intolerable interference with personal freedom. He writes: "This liberty consisted of active participation in collective power rather than the quiet enjoyment of individual independence. And indeed, in order to ensure such participation, it was necessary for the citizens to sacrifice this enjoyment in large measure. In the stage of development which we have now reached, it is absurd to demand such a sacrifice and impossible to obtain it." [9] He explains what he means by this "stage of development" in another passage: "The Ancients took more pleasure in their public life and less in their private: consequently, they sacrificed individual freedom to political liberty, sacrificing less to obtain more. Almost all modern man's pleasures are related to his private life: the vast majority, permanently excluded from power, inevitably has no more than a passing interest in its public life. Thus, if the moderns were to imitate the Ancients, they would sacrifice more to obtain less." [10] As regards the "vast majority permanently excluded from power," Constant points out that the Greek city-states were relatively small and simple social units in which individuals could make a direct and personal contribution to government, whereas we now live in large and complex industrial societies in which, at best, we are *collectively represented* in government and exert only an indirect influence on those who rule us.

Finally, Constant returned to the question of man's divided nature in his comparison between the Ancients and modern man. The Ancients lived during "the youth of the moral life," whereas we belong to its "maturity" or, more possibly, its "old age." The Ancients possessed a much more unified sensibility than our own, a greater homogeneity of character and temperament. They were single-minded—capable of lasting enthusiasm and total conviction—whereas we moderns are too self-aware and self-critical to achieve such easy conviction and moral self-confidence. Our preoccupation with ourselves makes us much more conscious of self-division and much more fearful of self-deception. "The Ancients experienced complete conviction about everything; there is scarcely anything about which our conviction is not weak, irresolute and of an incompleteness to which we try to blind ourselves." [11] Constant's picture of the ancient Greeks is of course simplified and idealized in the manner of his times. His characterization of his contemporaries is less easily refuted. The facts of serious self-division and continuous self-examination, which he projects from his knowledge of himself onto mankind at large, are what finally make it impossible for him to accept any doctrine which claims to ensure personal freedom by its "voluntary alienation" to a superior "general will." In fact this general will would in any case be interpreted and exercised, in the modern state, by men similarly divided between conflicting instincts and similarly lacking the single-minded moral vitality of civilization's youth. Given the tyranny and the crimes that have so often followed any major abdication of the individual to the collective will, freedom in all its forms, and individual freedom in particular, must be defended against attack from every quarter.

III Love

Constant's preoccupation with sexuality and love is second only to his concern for personal freedom and political liberty. His own statement of his "physical and moral" need of women has already been quoted and this was accompanied, as were all his actions and feelings, by a continual scrutiny of his motives and responses. Inevitably, such scrutiny produced further evidence of his divided nature, and he described himself in *Le Cahier rouge*, recalling his brief and youthful affair with Mme Trevor in 1785, as being both "excessively timid and wildly impulsive." [12] He goes on to say that at this stage in his life he had not yet learned that, in such matters, "one must take rather than ask." The learning of this lesson was by no means all gain, however. Indeed, it led him into a number of situations in which his sensitivity undermined his cynicism, in which he contracted obligations at variance with his desire for independence, and in which genuine affection sometimes interfered with the logic of libertinism.

Although he grew up in a libertine atmosphere, Constant's sensitive and introspective qualities encouraged in him an accompanying response to the more idealistic and romantic interpretations of love. He lived a sexual life divided between the cerebral stratagems of a Valmont and the sentimental effusions of a Werther. No doubt he reflected in his own personality something of that striking movement in European sensibility which occurred during his lifetime—the transition from eighteenth-century libertinism to early nineteenth-century romanticism. Constant saw these contrasting sexual attitudes, which he knew himself to possess, in national rather than historical terms. The preface to his French adaptation of Schiller's *Wallenstein*, which he wrote in 1809 and republished with some alterations in 1829, contains the following interesting passage:

We [i.e., the French] envisage love simply as a passion of the same nature as all human passions, so that its effect is to disorder our reason and its purpose to procure pleasure. The Germans see love as something religious, something sacred, an emanation of the divinity itself, a fulfillment of man's purpose on earth, a mysterious and all-powerful bond between two individuals whose whole existence is the one for the other. According to the first point of view, love is common to man and the animals; according to the second, it is common to man and God." [13]

A few lines later, Constant adds that "there is truth in both these conceptions." In fact, he experienced a recurrent conflict between the erotic and the ethical—a conflict which lies at the heart of *Adolphe*.

Given his natural timidity, his self-absorption, and his emphasis on privacy and independence, it is not surprising that Constant found it difficult to make satisfactory contact with others. This remains true despite his conversational brilliance and social success. On 6 July 1792, he wrote to Mme de Charrière: "I am detached from everything, nothing interests me, I am without moral ties . . ." [14] Later in the same letter he added: "I love my wife for 1,000 good qualities which she possesses, but the listlessness into which I am plunged has alienated her. When I experience a moment of closeness or warmth, she is either cold or casual and, in order to avoid an explanation that is beyond my power, I become silent and go away." [15] This particular problem of Constant's relations with Minna von Cramm may be no more than an example of ordinary temperamental differences, but his general experience of people confirmed his belief in the near-impossibility of true contact between individuals. However, although the failure of love in such instances emphasized the fact of ultimate separation, Constant believed that, ideally, love gave rise to the closest possible human ties and was the most effective answer available to the problem of human solitude and alienation. It is noticeable that in his moments of greatest happiness, with Mme de Charrière or Mme de Staël, what he emphasized above all was the "mutual understanding" existing between them, the many ties binding them together.

Such ties have another desirable effect. If love is the potential source of an intimacy which temporarily conquers solitude, it can also confer on the individual a feeling of significance and endurance within the general flux of time. One personality within Constant says that time conquers love, but another affirms that love conquers time. It can allay our lurking fear of human transience. It does this through building up, between two individuals, a store of memories based on difficulty and happiness shared together. Past and present are thus related, fused, and the relationship gives them significance and coherence. Time becomes a meaningful progression rather than a succession of undifferentiated or unrelated moments. Constant repeatedly emphasized the importance which the memory of earlier intimacies had for him. More than once it enabled him to replace a love affair that had ended by a genuine friendship. In the case of Charlotte von Hardenberg, whom he married in 1808, it led him to renew in 1804 a love affair which he thought had finished eleven years earlier.

It is largely the pre-Romantic in Constant, the admirer of the German identification of love with religiosity, that saw sexual passion as a means of surmounting the human condition. But there also existed within his nature a sometimes cynical and disillusioned realist remaining chiefly aware of the servitude of love and the clinging, stifling, emasculating influence of women. These two attitudes are not unexpected in such a self-divided person, but Constant's contradictory nature also led him to face other realities, particularly the frequently inseparable connection between love and suffering. Like his fictional hero Adolphe, he was inclined to embark on love affairs by calculation and for purely physical ends. The results of such enterprises were sometimes disconcertingly different from those intended. In some instances, after a purely cerebral exercise in seduction, he eventually fell, or believed himself to have fallen, genuinely in love. He now experienced the passion which he had originally merely simulated for tactical reasons. In those cases where his partner, on the other hand, continued to keep within the rules of the initial erotic ritual, the absence of a shared passion caused him acute suffering. At other times his own love died quickly, whereas the woman in question continued to love him with genuine passion. Here the absence of reciprocal love caused his partner to suffer, but he in turn experienced guilt and unhappiness at her distress (cf. the dilemma between Adolphe and Ellénore). In short, Constant simply discovered that there are many occasions when a love affair has little or nothing to do with a "marriage of true minds," and his writings abound in references to the coexistence of love and suffering.

In spite of his egoism, he was particularly sensitive to the suffering he sometimes inflicted on others and goes so far as to say, in the fictional context of *Adolphe*, that "the most ingenious metaphysical system cannot vindicate a man who breaks the heart of a woman who loved him." [16] He puts the problem in a less sentential way in some lines which occur, perhaps surprisingly, in his *Réflexions sur les constitutions* (1814) to which M. Georges Poulet has drawn attention:

Let us recall something which each of us has certainly experienced when, by force of circumstances, he took a decision that could cause intense suffering to someone other than himself. How many times, after having strengthened his resolve by rational argument, by calculation, and by a sense of real or imagined necessity, he has felt his firmness ebb away at the sight of the person whom he would cause to suffer, at the sight of the tears prompted by his first words! How many liaisons there are which continue for this reason only! How often egoism or prudence, considering themselves invincible while they are on their own, give way before a physical presence! [17]

Sensitivity to the suffering of others, then, and particularly to suffering caused by our own failure to love, is a natural human quality and sometimes strong enough to make us change our minds. The depth of such sensitivity is affected, according to Constant, by our own experience of wretchedness which "teaches us to feel for others." It is perhaps the suffering caused to others by unhappy love, rather than love as such, which makes the greatest demands on our humanity.

It was one of Constant's many very human qualities that he did not always live up to the requirements of his own ideals. He found it extremely difficult, sometimes impossible, to curb his own egoism, especially in his love affairs. His autobiographical writings contain some engaging confessions of failure. At the same time, he was aware that the question of personal freedom, to which he was so genuinely devoted, is beset by many problems in the sphere of sexual love. We have seen that love, ideally conceived, can be interpreted as a means by which the individual seeks to transcend the limits of his individuality. We have also seen that love on a more workaday level—and particularly when it is not a balanced and reciprocal relationship—can lead to a clash between contending freedoms. Constant thus found it necessary to introduce into his thinking about freedom and love the additional idea of renunciation. There is obviously a sense in which we are not genuinely free unless we are capable of working against our own instincts and desires. Constant understood this, understood that "freedom feeds on sacrifice," and attempted to put his theory into practice by acts of renunciation calculated to lessen the suffering of others. On 12 July 1808, he wrote to Mme de Nassau: "I am convinced that true morality involves a maximum effort to spare others from suffering, and that we have a duty to sacrifice to this end not only our own happiness but even, in some measure, outward appearance and people's good opinion." [18] The length of Constant's stormy relationship with Mme de Staël resulted, in part, from his determination to put this principle into practice, even if he was also understandably intimidated by the formidable Germaine's violent anger. No doubt it was the experience of this liaison, as much as anything else, which convinced him that personal freedom remains a moral problem beyond the reach of purely social or political arrangements.

IV *Pessimism*

One would scarcely expect Constant to be an optimist, given his self-accusing nature, the unhappiness or frustration of most of his love affairs, and the spectacle which he witnessed of individual freedom being menaced in turn by the French Revolution, Napoleonic dictatorship, and a backward-looking monarchy. In fact, however, his pessimism—while it obviously had temperamental origins and was intensified by external events—was, above all, metaphysical in character. From an early age, he was acutely conscious of the brevity of human life, the inevitability of death, and these facts, which have stimulated intensity of living in many people, often produced in Constant something approaching that listlessness and torpor which the Greeks called *akedeia*. Mention has already been made of his timidity, his procrastination, his frequent moods of deep gloom. If such attitudes were encouraged by intense self-absorption, they were further stimulated by a conviction that the inescapable prospect of death robs life, as lived from day to day, of significant differentiation or value. Whatever the activities in which we indulge, and whatever their temporary meaning for us, they are experienced within a wider framework of senseless uniformity: "One day is the same as another and any hour today resembles exactly the same hour yesterday. Time flows by and, apart from my work which is progressing, I cannot render a particular moment distinguishable from those which preceded it and those which will follow." [19] These lines were written in 1812 and confirm a striking expression of *akedeia* written to Mme de Charrière twenty-two years earlier: ". . . man cannot get it into his head once and for all that it is not worthwhile worrying about today since we must die tomorrow. Thomson, the author of *The Seasons*, often spent whole days in bed and when asked why he did not get up replied: 'I see no motive to rise, man.' Nor do I. I see no motive for anything in this world and I have no taste for anything." [20] One other uncompromising expression, among many, of this deep personal pessimism is found in a letter written a year later:

Perhaps it is my misfortune to feel too strongly . . . that all our pursuits, all our efforts, all we attempt or do or change, are mere momentary games leading only to imminent annihilation. Therefore we have no more incentive for winning fame, for conquering an empire, for writing a good book, than we have for taking a walk or playing whist. Time flows at a steady rate quite independently of us and bears us away whether we wake or sleep, whether we are active or totally passive. This ordinary, but constantly forgotten, truth is always in the forefront of my mind and makes me almost indifferent to everything.[21]

The fact of human mortality, then, makes life both ultimately meaningless and immediately monotonous for Constant. At a theoretical level, he reacted to experience with the passivity of one who envisages at most the possibility of stoical acceptance.

His pessimism, in this respect, was close to that of such near-contemporaries as Leopardi and Vigny. At this point too, it is different from that of a twentieth-century writer such as Camus. Camus regarded his own analysis of the "absurdity" of human existence as the necessary basis on which could be built a new, positive interpretation of life and of the individual's role in it. Temperamentally, too, he reacted differently, claiming that his "horror of dying" coexisted with an "intense appetite for living." Constant responded to this state of affairs in what is almost the opposite direction. His political activities, his love affairs, his compulsive gambling, his seven volumes on religious experience, can all be seen—and probably ought to be seen—as attempts to escape the consequences of his own inner void, as textbook examples of that feverish effort to ignore metaphysical solitude which Pascal analysed in the *Pensées* and named *divertissement* or "distraction."

The fact that Constant had no panacea to offer, together with the fact that considerable sharpness of mind accompanied his pessimism, ends by making him appear a more modern figure than has perhaps been suggested so far. If he is quite distant in his ideas from the Camus of *La Peste*, he is often very close to the later, and more desperate, Camus of *La Chute*. There is also an echo in his writing of Malraux's analysis of the twentieth-century "death of man" which followed the nineteenth-century "death of God." The following passage from the first volume of *De la religion considérée dans sa source, ses formes et ses développements* (*On Religion . . .*) (1824), although it was written with particular reference to the post-1789 situation in France, has a striking, modern relevance in its skepticism, its shrewd antitheses, and its awareness of historical and moral dislocation:

Man congratulates himself on having rejected all prejudices, all errors, all fears, yet all fears, prejudices and errors seem to be unleashed. The rule of reason has been proclaimed and the whole world has been struck by madness. All systems are based on deliberate thought, directed towards individual advantage, allow pleasure and advise rest; yet never was wild behavior more shameful, agitation more unruly, and suffering more acute. Skepticism, in its attacks on established order, which it has reduced to dust, has cast a slur on feelings which humanity cannot do without. As he emerges victoriously from his battles, man gazes on a world bereft of protective powers and remains thunderstruck by his own success. He is no longer sustained by things which earlier filled him with enthusiasm—the excitement of the struggle, the idea of dangers bravely confronted, the thirst to win disputed rights. His imagination, once preoccupied by the thought of successes which were still denied him, and now inactive and lacking substance, turns in upon itself. He is alone on the earth which will inevitably swallow him up. On this earth the different generations follow one another, transient, contingent, and isolated; they appear, they suffer, they die, and no bond holds them together. No voice still sounds, from the generations that have disappeared, to address those that are now living; and the voice of those now living must soon be engulfed by the same eternal silence. What will man do, without memory and without hope, placed between an abandoned past and a sealed-off future? His cries are no longer heard and his prayers remain unanswered. He has rejected all the support with which his predecessors surrounded him and is dependent on his own strength. With this strength he must face satiety, old age, remorse, and the innumerable evils which afflict him. In this extreme and unnatural situation his actions continually rebut his rational arguments and his fears are an unceasing expiation of his derision. He seems to be the victim of a double folly, at one moment insulting what he reveres and at another trembling before the very thing he has trampled underfoot." [22]

Constant makes two major points here. He considers that man has destroyed a set of established, traditional values, but has shown himself incapable of replacing them by new values which possess meaning and bring satisfaction. He also claims, perhaps more significantly, that post-1789 man has created a new intellectual and social situation which cuts him off from the culture of the past, from the voice which spoke on behalf of "the generations that have disappeared." No doubt the revolution of 1789 appeared, and indeed was, a dramatic break in cultural continuity so that Constant regarded modern man not only as solitary in a metaphysical sense, but also as historically isolated. This is another reason why his pessimism has a certain modern ring. Today we share Constant's feeling of being increasingly cut off from our inheritance—though in our case we attribute this primarily to the astonishingly accelerated rate of technological and social change which has occurred in the last sixty years. Whatever the reason, we have experienced the lack of contact between generations to which he refers; indeed, so fast is the rate of change that large gaps are now opening up between decades, let alone between generations.

And yet, despite the drama of human alienation and confusion which he described so convincingly, Constant's pessimism did not prevent him from living a life in which he attempted, in some cases with considerable success, to achieve public ends and realize personal objectives. It is true that a certain temperamental pessimism made him depressed or indecisive in much that he did, but he neither committed suicide nor withdrew into complete isolation. Apart from the fact that so many thinkers have made of their pessimism a philosophical theory or a literary theme (and to this extent have not genuinely lived its consequences), we can see, in the passage from *De la religion* quoted above, intellectual reasons for Constant's continued activity and some justification for his not following the most severe logic to be associated with the fact of human mortality. His pessimistic analysis of modern man quite clearly rested on a set of implied values or standards. It was precisely because of his contemporaries' insensitivity to these standards that he found himself criticizing them so severely. In other words, despite his consciousness of human mortality and his belief that, logically, it puts the conquest of empire or a game of whist on the same meaningless level, Constant continued to live by certain human values which he clarified and defended in much of his work as politician, historian of religion, and writer. As a politician, he campaigned for freedom and liberty. As an historian of religion, he tried to demonstrate the narrow inadequacy of a purely rational attitude to life. As a writer, he attempted to define a new conception of literature, a literature which would deal more truthfully and more comprehensively with the nature of human beings and their personal relationships.

CHAPTER 2

Politics and Revolution

THE cataclysm of the French Revolution, occurring as it did when Constant was still in his early twenties, ensured that his political theory and practice took precedence—chronologically, as well as in terms of their importance for his contemporaries—over his activities as historian of religion and man of letters. It is clear that his general intellectual formation was strongly influenced by the ideals of the Enlightenment—rationalism, tolerance, freedom of thought—and while it is true that the Enlightenment lacked a coherent and systematic political theory, its ideals encouraged political liberalism and affected Constant's position to this extent. At the same time, modern historians are generally agreed that a direct link between Enlightenment ideals and the course of the Revolution is not easily established. We shall therefore not be surprised to find, in Constant's early political activities and writings, a complex attitude of enthusiasm and reserve, of approval and qualification, which aroused antagonism among extremists of both revolution and reaction.

I Early Attitudes

The available evidence is thin and scattered concerning Constant's early political ideas. We have already seen, however, that a deep love of freedom was an enduring feature of his temperament. We would therefore expect him to sympathize instinctively with political liberalism and may note that he was pro-Whig and anti-Tory as early as his stay in Edinburgh between 1783 and 1785. Something of his liberal reputation within the family is suggested by his cousin, Charles de Constant. The latter, writing in 1794 of Benjamin's period of service at the Court of Brunswick from 1788 onward, commented: "I have never understood what he was doing at Brunswick, and still less what it is to be a gentleman of the chamber to a despotic duke when one is born a republican and shares the feelings and opinions of republicanism." [1] In fact, Constant was mockingly critical in his attitude to the Duke's court. Although the Duke of Brunswick was regarded as an enlightened ruler, Constant found the atmosphere in Brunswick stiflingly petty and the court customs heavily Germanic.

It was also during his service in Brunswick that Constant gave further evidence of his general political position—and earned the title of "the Swiss Jacobin"—by reading and reacting to Burke's *Reflections on the French Revolution* (first published in 1790 and translated into French in the same year). As early as October, 1789, he had commented with satisfaction on the news from France, whereas Burke regarded the fall of the Bastille as heralding calamity. Burke had a strong feeling for the established order and believed that true progress could be made only by the improvement, rather than the demolition, of existing social structures. He interpreted the Revolution as an attack on the twin foundations of society—religion and landed property—and his devotion to the rule of law was shocked by the popular violence and wanton cruelty of 1789–90. It is not surprising, in these circumstances, that Constant should have written in December, 1790, to Mme de Charrière:

I am currently busy reading and refuting Burke's book against the French *levellers*. This famous book contains as many absurdities as it does lines, and thus it is highly successful in all English and German circles. He defends the nobility, the exclusion of the *sectaires*,[2] the establishment of a dominant religion, and other things of this nature. . . . I believe, as you do, that what we are witnessing is fundamentally knavery and fury. But I prefer the knavery and fury which overthrow citadels, destroy titles and similar follies, and place all religions on an equal footing, to those which seek to preserve and hallow these wretched monstrosities of barbarous Jewish stupidity grafted onto the ignorant ferocity of the Vandals. Inevitably, the human race is born stupid and led by scoundrels. But as between scoundrels and scoundrels, I vote for the Mirabeaus and Barnaves rather than the Sartines and Breteuils.[3]

These comments have given rise to a good deal of debate. Their main interest lies in the fact that they indicate a conscious choice between evils on Constant's part. His republicanism was deeply, even passionately, held, but he was not blind to the faults and excesses of the revolutionaries. As the Revolution continued on its course, he felt increasingly obliged to take sides in the way his letter indicates and showed some sympathy with the Girondins—a less extreme left-wing group than the Jacobins and a significant force in the new Legislative Assembly of 1791. Nevertheless, as the drama of the Revolution unfolded, it became more and more difficult to maintain an unvarying position. Constant experienced, in fact, the familiar dilemma of the liberal faced by extreme political polarization and his views vacillated a good deal from 1793 onward.

II *Vacillations*

One of the important ideas in Burke's *Reflections* was his argument that the French Revolution represented an attempt to replace an imperfect but humanly attainable state of affairs by one which was theoretically perfect but unattainable in practice. He saw the fearful possibilities, in terms of violence and terrorism, of ideological abstraction, and raised the whole question of the potentialities, for good and evil alike, of human nature. Ironically, particularly in view of his dismissive comments on Burke, Constant now found himself wrestling with these very problems of individual freedom and state terror, idealistic ends and inhumane means. By 1793 the whole political picture had changed dramatically. France appeared to be threatened by dissident groups within the country, supported by the counterrevolutionary activities of *émigré* groups on her borders; Prussia had declared war on France (July, 1792); violent mob rule culminated in the September Massacres when hundreds of priests, political prisoners, and common-law criminals were murdered with great brutality; in January, 1793, Louis XVI was executed and later in the same year the Committee of Public Safety organized the Terror which reached a pitch of intensity in June and July, 1794 (between 10 June and 27 July there were 1,376 executions in Paris alone).

Events such as these were bound to cause Constant much concern. In one sense they may have confirmed his more pessimistic views on human nature, but they were also an affront to his feeling for constitutional government, his republican idealism, his rationalism, his belief in individual liberty, and his dislike of violence. The complexity of events and of the ideas behind them caused him to react in a number of different ways ranging from horror and gloom to irony or attempted justification. His letters to Mme de Charrière in October, 1793, show his dislike of the Convention—the new assembly which lasted from September, 1792, to November, 1795—and he is equally severe in his condemnation of the "infamous" Paris Commune and the "execrable" Jacobins. At the same time, he continued to disagree with Mme de Charrière's monarchical views. At a moment when she was hesitating between the moderate monarchism of Mallet du Pan and the more reactionary royalism of Ferrand, he claimed to experience no difficulties of choice since he rejected the ideas of both men. He desired a peaceful, nonviolent republic, however, and added: "If new Marats and Robespierres, etc., arise to disturb it [the republic] and are not crushed immediately they appear, I shall abandon humanity and abjure the name of man."[4]

A particularly revealing letter is one which Constant dated 16, 17, 18 October 1793 and which he wrote, during an illness, to Mme de Charrière. He begins by expressing his stupefaction and horror at the behavior of the mob, dancing, singing, and applauding as they accompanied victims to the guillotine and witnessed their execution. *Quel peuple!* he exclaims, reports that more than sixty départements (a total of eighty-three had been created in 1789) have demanded the Queen's death, and observes that neither the Greeks nor the Romans displayed such cruelty to their fellows as that shown by the French masses. At the same time, he hopes that this is a passing phenomenon, being unable to believe that the French are so exceptionally ferocious. Continuing his letter the following day, Constant is in a more optimistic mood having reread eyewitness accounts of the atrocities committed in America during the War of Independence. Following a series of barbaric acts which he likens to those of the Convention, he points out that America became "a free, peaceful and happy country." He goes further and suggests to Mme Charrière that they would both find it instructive if they were to draw up a list of crimes committed after the fall of the Bastille by aristocrats on the one hand and revolutionaries on the other. Still continuing his letter on the third day, Constant alters his tone once more. The news of several setbacks for the Revolutionary Army in its campaign against the First Coalition makes him admit that, having deplored the atrocities of the Convention for two days, he is now deploring its defeats. He might still be tempted to side with the European Coalition, but he realizes that, if they finally won, the European powers would impose a right-wing despotism and encourage all the old restrictions and superstitions. Dictatorship by the followers of Ferrand would be no improvement on that of Robespierre.

This last remark makes it particularly clear that Constant's "middle" position, his rejection of both extremes, was the inevitable outcome of his devotion to political liberty and individual freedom. At the end of his letter, he invokes America as the land of liberty and declares that, if liberty dies in Europe, he will seek peace and freedom in the New World.

III *Moving Left*

Shortly after the writing of the long letter summarized above, Constant's political ideas underwent another change, and his sympathies moved more clearly in the direction of the Jacobins, even of Robespierre. Here again his devotion to freedom was a factor. There is evidence to suggest that he grew increasingly tired of war, longed for peace, and began to argue that peace was an essential prerequisite of liberty. It now seemed that only the Jacobin group in the Convention had the energy and singleness of mind—particularly since the fall of the Girondins—to bring peace both to the interior of the country and to its borders with neighboring states. At the level of practical politics, therefore, he began to regard the Jacobins as being at least a necessary evil and the eventual means to the ends he sought. There were even occasions, during 1794, when he expressed admiration for Robespierre before the latter's overthrow by the moderates in the Convention.

Two other factors, one intellectual and one more emotional, also played their part in Constant's change of emphasis. At the intellectual level he began to discern in the progress of the Revolution a certain inescapable logic. He even sketched (but did not complete) the outlines of an imaginary conversation between Louis XVI, Marat (the organizer of the September Massacres) and Brissot (whose followers led the campaign against priests and *émigrés*). The effect of this conversation was to show that certain factors made revolution and bloodshed inseparable. By the same logic, the early executions inevitably led to others and, eventually, to the killing of some of the leading executors themselves. This kind of analysis, even in such embryonic form, allows one to draw a number of very different conclusions. Constant, who had witnessed the mounting violence and terror, chose to argue—at least for a short period—that the logic of bloodshed and tyranny would have to run its course before new hopes could be realized or a new direction taken.

The second factor which affected Constant's views at this time was his final stay at the Court of Brunswick in 1794. We have already noted his reputation there, some years earlier, as a "Swiss Jacobin," and his position now became all but intolerable. Events in Paris, together with the war between France and Prussia, had created a bitterly counterrevolutionary atmosphere at the court. This was intensified by the presence of aristocratic *émigrés* whose ideas outraged Constant. In general, the court did not hide its hostility toward his liberal ideas, and he seems to have begun to adopt some of the more extreme positions which his political enemies attributed to him. Something of this is suggested in his note to Mme de Charrière: "To will the end is to will the means, and I am tired of my inconsistency." [5]

It is characteristic of all attitudes of political "realism" that they are subject to sudden alteration by events. Constant's newfound revolutionary realism was no exception. In June and July, the more moderate elements within the Convention united successfully against Robespierre. On 9 Thermidor [6] (27 July) he was arrested, and next day he and more than twenty of his supporters were executed. Shortly afterward another notorious terrorist, Carrier, was tried and put to death. Gradually, the machine of terror was put into reverse, the Convention reasserted its power, and Jacobin policies were increasingly repudiated.

The events of 9 Thermidor marked the beginning of the end of revolution. As one historian puts it: "The fall of Robespierre is the dramatic crisis of the Revolution, the solution, in the high and primitive sense of the phrase, of its intrigue. The French Republic is not to be the Republic of Virtue. From now on something lofty, inhuman, terrible has gone out of the Revolution. Men have returned to their everyday virtues and vices. Common sense and common foolishness have resumed sway. The Thermidorean reaction has begun." [7] It was this "Thermidorean reaction" which enabled Constant to believe afresh in the attainment of his own political ideals of republicanism and liberty by means much more in keeping with his own essentially moderate views and constitutional convictions. The turn of public events made the prospect of a direct role in politics seem more attractive; it also enabled him to share, in large measure, the ideas of Mme de Staël, whom he first met in September, 1794. Some months earlier their ideas would have been irreconcilable but by 1795, during the constitutional transition from the Convention to the Directory, both were in Paris and largely in agreement about their political ideals.

IV   *From Convention to Directory*

Benjamin Constant and Mme de Staël arrived together in Paris on 25 May 1795. Within weeks an important political debate had developed round the question of a proposed new constitution—the so-called Constitution of the Year III. Briefly, the committee charged with the task of drawing up a constitution proposed an Executive, consisting of five Directors who would have power to appoint ministers, would control the army and navy, be responsible for foreign policy, but have no voice in legislation. The Legislature was to consist of two chambers: a *Conseil des 500* with a minimum age of thirty and a *Conseil des anciens* (250 deputies whose minimum age was to be forty-five— a kind of upper chamber). The five Directors were to be chosen, by the *Conseil des anciens*, from a list of fifty names proposed by the *Conseil des 500*.

With the new antirevolutionary feeling in the country, the seats of many deputies in the old Convention now seemed unsafe. Rumors circulated that the deputies were therefore contemplating an amendment to the draft constitution (it was in fact brought forward and passed on 18 August) by which two-thirds of the Convention's members would automatically become members of the new Legislature. Constant joined in the resulting controversy, writing three anonymous *Lettres à un député de la Convention.*[8]

The moderates, including Mme de Staël, were opposed to what seemed an attempt at self-perpetuation on the part of the Convention. Constant's three letters, published in the *Nouvelles*

politiques, nationales et étrangères of 24, 25, and 26 June 1795,
argued the case against the amendment. All three letters were
essentially about tactics. Constant was concerned with the health
and solidity of the republic; he favored the arrangements which
he considered most likely to secure this end. In the first letter,
he accuses the deputies of wishing to act in the manner of
royalists, of lacking faith in the judgment of the electorate, of
seeking an arbitrary and despotic route to power. He understands
the fear which motivates the Convention but insists: ". . . fear
is short-sighted; do not let yourself be blinded by it." Only by
legitimate reelection can they sit with dignity, and be held in
honor, in the new assembly.

In the second letter, he comes back to the question of fear—
the deputies' fear of reprisals for their past excesses by an assembly of more moderate successors—and writes: "You are mistaken,
my friend. It is precisely by presenting themselves as accused
persons who fear judgment and who, in order to avoid it, occupy
the judges' seats themselves; it is by retaining power not as a
means of public good but as an instrument of self-defense, that
the Convention would perish." [9]

In the third letter, we have the more practical argument that
if, as a result of electoral defeat, most of the old deputies are
"reabsorbed into the mass of the people," they will fare better
than would those, much smaller in number and more vulnerable
to reprisals, who will have to give up their seats under the terms
of the proposed amendment. He adds: "Thus in terms of your
own interest, as well as in the name of the republic; on behalf
of the members who would be retained in the assembly, as well
as on behalf of those who would be excluded, I beseech you to
renounce an idea which, on the frivolous pretext of a precarious
and illusory safety, would be a terrible confession of your fears
and your remorse and which, on account of the universal dis-
approval to which it would undoubtedly give rise, would create
the very danger which you delude yourself into thinking you
will escape." [10]

Constant's letters aroused quick and positive reactions from
both ends of the political spectrum. The royalists congratulated
the author—his identity probably revealed by Mme de Staël—
and Constant later described his sense of outrage when a committee of writers sent a spokesman to invite him to join them

in working for the reestablishment of the monarchy.[11] He began to realize that his letters were ill-judged, in terms of practical politics, and that he had underestimated the continuing vulnerability of the young republic. Within weeks of the publication of his letters, and despite the acceptance on 18 August of the amendment which they attacked, the royalists displayed considerable power and cohesion, profited from the weakness of the regular army, and were defeated only by the young Bonaparte's famous "whiff of grapeshot" on 13 Vendémiaire (4 October).

The left, on the other hand, had realized the danger from the start and the Girondin Louvet—ironically a friend of Constant's—had vehemently attacked the anonymous letters as expressions of impudent folly and royalist effrontery. The whole episode provided, in fact, an important lesson for Constant. A growing royalist movement might have overthrown the regime in free elections and paved the way for the very thing he disliked most—some form of monarchical restoration. He learned the hard truth that ethical quality and political reality can be in direct and irreducible conflict. As he stated much later: "In 1795 the Convention was like Bonaparte's Senate in 1814, a defense of blood and mud raised against the partisans of the *ancien régime*. It was a sordid defense, but one which had to be preserved." [12] In fact, at the end of October, the Convention declared an amnesty for all political offenses committed since the establishment of the republic. It also declared its own dissolution (though with two-thirds of its members retained under the new constitution). The Directory replaced it in November and lasted for the next four years.

V   *Defending the Directory*

In the previous July, Constant had written and signed a long letter to the editor of the *Républicain français* beginning with the characteristic sentence: *Le malheur a toujours quelque chose de sacré*,[13] and pleading for the return to France not of the original aristocratic *émigrés*, but of those who were fugitives —through a true love of liberty—from later revolutionary excesses. This was linked with a general plea that all moderates should rally to the defense of the republic. About the same time, Mme de Staël had written her *Réflexions sur la paix intérieure* which made a similar plea for cooperation between moderates of both right and left. As it turned out, the composition and policy of the new Directory met Constant's wishes in a number of ways. It represented essentially middle-class government—uncompromisingly republican, but as far removed from Jacobin extremism as from monarchism. Voting was again on a property basis and it has been suggested that this, together with the American-style two-chamber arrangement, appealed particularly to Constant.

The first weeks of the new government's existence, however, brought him little satisfaction [14] and culminated in the denunciation of Mme de Staël (not without some reason) as an alien intriguer. Following a government expulsion order, she left Paris, accompanied by Benjamin, on 21 December 1795 and retired to Coppet. It was here that Constant proceeded to write his first major political pamphlet. He returned to Paris on his own in April, 1796, and, among other things, publicized his pamphlet to which he had given the explicit title, *De la force du gouvernement actuel de la France et de la nécessité de s'y rallier.*

This new work was in many ways a continuation and elaboration of the article published nearly twelve months earlier in the *Républicain français.* As in Constant's other political writings of this period, it contains a somewhat uncertain mixture of practical argument and abstract principle. It also offers an eloquent defense of the republican government of the Directory and advocates a middle position equally inimical to terrorism and royalism. Because of the growing royalist movement, particular trouble is taken to reject the monarchist position. There are eight chapters, including the conclusion, and there is in addition a short preface in which the tone of the work is set by the statement: "Order and liberty are on one side, anarchy and despotism on the other." Anarchy and despotism are the fruits of terrorism and monarchy respectively and must be opposed; order and liberty are enshrined in the policies of the Directory which thus merits the support of all men of goodwill and moderation.

Chapter 1 reveals Constant's sharp change of attitude since his three letters of June, 1795. Significantly, this chapter is entitled "Des hommes qui ont attaqué la Convention" and argues, in effect, that the moderate majority in the Convention rightly sought to maintain power as its only defense and was wrongly attacked for doing so. While there is political realism in this view, Constant hardly sustains it shortly afterward when he moves on to a characteristic moral generalization: "It is by praising men that one encourages them toward the good; it is by showing oneself to be convinced that they cannot resist honest deeds that one obliges them to perform these deeds." [15] Nevertheless, there are subtle arguments in this chapter and the tone throughout is firm and uncompromising.

The second chapter argues that if the government is strongly attacked by the antirepublican right, it will inevitably attract to its defense extremist terrorists of the left who will subsequently dominate it. Constant makes it clear that he supports the Directory because of the ideal which it enshrines as well as the power which it wields, and he concludes: "Men of all persuasions! . . . rally to the support of a government which offers you peace and liberty, and which will bury you beneath its ruins if it collapses." [16]

In Chapter 3 Constant lists the *maux actuels de la France*—a series of military, social, and economic ills. Somewhat simplistically, he attributes them to the Revolution only, not to the republican government. He asserts that no form of monarchical government would lessen these evils—if anything, it would increase them—and he claims that enthusiasm for liberty (republicanism) can perform miracles whereas monarchism cannot. It is in the interests of the Directory to lessen these evils, whereas a restored monarchy would find political advantage in intensifying them. The present stability of the Directory mitigates the sometimes bloodthirsty past of the republic; the monarchy would exploit this terroristic past and use it as an excuse for imposing a despotic present.

This last argument was not without its difficulties from Constant's point of view. It required him to minimize past terror in praising the Directory, yet to emphasize this same terror in warning against royalist vengeance. In fact, the argument does not work very satisfactorily, and we find Constant obliged by it to refer, not very convincingly, to "the small number of actions with which one reproaches the first moments of a republic seeking to establish itself." [17] It is consistent with this third chapter generally that Constant should be careful to draw lessons from the experience of the "White Terror" and to emphasize the dangers of royalist vengeance.

The very brief Chapter 4 sees that there are some categories of men whose adherence to the republic cannot reasonably be demanded (those who lost all that was dearest to them—their closest relatives and their whole way of life—during the Revolution). It is argued in Chapter 5 that a resurgence of revolutionary terror is an illusory fear. Happily, says Constant, the stronger the government becomes the more conciliatory it shows itself to be. The freedom of the press has been established and dangerous power has been removed from suspect hands. To those who argue that a major state cannot retain its status and be a republic, Constant replies in Chapter 6 that the new experiment must be given time; any conclusion that the experiment has failed is still premature.

The last two chapters offer a more positive defense of republicanism. It is clear that Constant closely associates this form of constitution with his ideals of freedom and equality under the law, and that he believes strongly in representative democracy. In Chapter 7 he also argues in favor of the *mobile* nature of republicanism—it is an historically inevitable movement forward toward liberty and progress—just as he condemns what he considers to be the *static* nature of monarchism. He writes: "Emerging from an impenetrable cloud which covers its birth, we see the human race advancing toward equality over the debris of institutions of all kinds." [18] And there are echoes of Mme de Staël and anticipations of Chateaubriand in a longer passage prompted by the idea of inactivity and purposelessness—something very like the *mal du siècle*—which he associates with monarchism:

. . . this inactivity is the source of one of our greatest misfortunes, of a misfortune which is not only political but individual, of that arid and consuming feeling which devours our existence, drains all objects of color and, like the burning winds of Africa, withers and blights everything it meets. This feeling, for which no word exists either in the ancient languages or in that of the only modern European nation which was free before the French, chiefly arises from a deprivation of aims, interests and hopes other than narrow, personal ones. It pursues not only the obscure citizens of a monarchy, but kings on their thrones and ministers in their palaces, because the soul is always constricted when it is driven into egoism.[19]

Constant concludes with an attack on arbitrary power and a plea for strict legality and adherence to principles. He argues that any friend of liberty must be a friend of the government of the Directory, but only so long as those who govern avoid the temptation of arbitrary behavior and "certain revolutionary habits." While he retains confidence in the Directory, he reminds its members that the greatest evil experienced by France since 1789, and the most difficult evil to counteract, is ironically enough an impatient desire to do good. He adds, with characteristic insight and sharpness, that it is infinitely more dangerous to set up a revolution on behalf of virtue than one on behalf of crime. Here, as at several important points in the pamphlet, he combines general principles and practical realism in a way that distinguishes the best political writing—writing devoted to the art of the possible.

Naturally enough, *De la force du gouvernement actuel* was well received in official quarters. It was widely reviewed, and republished in *Le Moniteur* (1–9 May) on the orders of the government. Inevitably, it also attracted some severe attacks from right-wing reviewers including the journalist Louis-François Bertin (Bertin de Veaux). The offensively personal tone of the latter's article in *La Feuille du jour* of 15 June led to his being challenged to a duel by Constant. The actual duel was averted by the intervention of a friend of both men. Bertin de Veaux withdrew his remarks. He had written about Constant from hearsay only and under the impression that he was a dangerous terrorist.

The attacks on Constant as a "foreigner," the banning of Mme de Staël from France, and the further measures taken against foreigners by the Directory after the Babeuf conspiracy, were all factors in Benjamin's decision to seek French nationality. He pointed to existing legislation making French citizenship available to descendants of families driven from France in earlier times by religious persecution (such was his own position). He also emphasized that he had invested two-thirds of his limited fortune in France and reminded the government of his repeated support of the Convention and the republican cause. In 1796, on his return to Switzerland, he wrote an article entitled "De la restitution des droits politiques aux descendants des religionnaires fugitifs," and he was eventually granted French nationality in 1798. By this time his reputation was established as a political theorist whose republicanism distinguished him from the right while his emphasis on individual freedom, his feeling for property and his sense of social order separated him from the more extreme left. He was, in fact, the archetypal middle-of-the-road liberal.

VI *Three further Pamphlets*

In the two years following the publication of *De la force du gouvernement actuel*, Constant wrote several pamphlets of considerable political interest. The first and most important, *Des réactions politiques*, was published in March 1797.[20] This was a more theoretical, less circumstantial, work than *De la force du gouvernement actuel*. It scrutinized, in a rather formalist manner, the nature of political reaction, some general political principles, arbitrary government, and the relationship between them. To this extent it reexamined, at a more abstract and analytical level, issues already touched on in the brochure of the previous year. The central role given by Constant to the unswerving application of certain crucial political principles is particularly important because of the related assumption that a rational organization of society is both desirable and possible. This is an assumption denied by right-wing theorists of the period, and notably by Burke. Constant, on the contrary, argued that such concepts as freedom and justice must be carefully defined and then systematically applied by continual reference to principle rather than circumstantial calculation. This pamphlet is the work of the natural constitution-builder in Constant, as distinct from the practising politician.

Something of the flavor of the work is conveyed by the opening analysis of political reaction. Constant defines revolution as the means by which political and social institutions are brought into harmony with a changed set of ideas enjoying widespread popular support. Once institutions are made to correspond to prevailing ideas in this way, peace and order are reestablished and revolution ends successfully and satisfactorily (Constant instances Switzerland, Holland, and America). However, if revolutionary action exceeds the agreed range of ideas and goes on to realize others which enjoy less general approval, a counter-revolution or political *reaction* is provoked.

Obviously this analysis is open to criticism—if only because the instinctively middle-of-the-road Constant comes close to contradiction by seeking to define revolution in terms of moderation. In fact, his definition of revolution hardly distinguishes it clearly enough from other forms of political change. Furthermore, he leaves unspecified the criteria by which one would judge whether or not certain ideas enjoy sufficiently wide popular support to justify revolutionary action. Indeed, many revolutions have begun at least as minority movements. However Constant's assumptions, though of doubtful validity, enable him to claim that the French Revolution, originally a rejection of privilege, went on to attack property more generally and consequently provoked a severe reaction. Political reaction of this kind adopts, in its turn, passion rather than rationality and arbitrary decision rather than legality. Hence the danger, inherent in political reaction, of bloodshed, crime, and injustice.

All this is very partial, despite an air of detached, reasoned analysis. Little or nothing is said of the crimes and injustices associated with revolution itself, and Constant uses most of the remaining chapters to discuss means of counteracting reactionary ideas. He outlines the duties of a republican government faced with pressure from right-wing personalities and ideas. He also expands on the special role of writers and intellectuals and their duty to defend liberal ideas. He regrets that many contemporary writers are not sufficiently active in defense of the republic and argues that the massacres committed by certain revolutionaries are often wrongly attributed by intellectuals to revolutionary ideology rather than to the criminal tendencies of particular individuals. While still on the subject of writers, however, Constant shows his basic moderation by maintaining that, while he detests those who attack freedom, he also scorns those who sully freedom by the manner in which they defend it.

The seventh chapter contains an interesting discussion of the freedom of the press. Constant is also refreshingly aware of the widespread human tendency to support principles only—or actively only—when they benefit one's own cause or are apparently being betrayed by one's opponents. On the wider issue of general principles as such, a general principle is defined as the result which always follows a given combination of events or ideas. In other words, a general principle is not strictly abstract, but tied eventually to concrete circumstances. In addition, a distinction is made between primary and secondary principles. The existence of the latter again facilitates an empirical application of the former. For Constant, then, arbitrary power amounts to the disregarding of principles. The arbitrary is seen as destructive in its efforts—in science, morals, and politics alike —and in the sphere of politics Constant defines the Terror as arbitrary rule taken to extremes. Arbitrary government is, indeed, "the great enemy of all freedom, the corrupting vice of all institutions, the germ of death which can neither be modified nor mitigated, but which must be destroyed." [21] On the following page, Constant again displays his fundamental constitutionalism, referred to earlier, when he writes: "A constitution is the guarantee of a people's liberty; consequently, everything which has to do with liberty is constitutional and consequently, also nothing is constitutional which is not related to liberty." [22] Proper principles, then, enshrined in a constitution, provide the only effective guarantee against both arbitrary power and counterrevolutionary reaction.

The first edition of *Des réactions politiques*, published in March, was soon sold out and the second edition, which appeared in May, was prefaced by an additional essay entitled *Des effets de la Terreur*.[23] This was mainly a reply to an article by Adrien de Lezay claiming that the Terror had been a necessary element in the establishment of the republic. Constant's essay is in some ways a counterweight to *Des réactions politiques*, saying that "the Terror was not necessary for the salvation of the republic." It is an attack on Jacobinism and makes the important point that systematic terror—terror as an ideological principle—is "much more horrible than the brutal and ferocious violence of individual terrorists." Constant goes so far as to blame the Terror (no doubt with considerable justification) for various counterrevolutionary manifestations in 1793—the rising in Lyon, the rebellion of the Vendée, etc. To accept crime, and thus grant an amnesty to the past, is also to corrupt the future.

The third pamphlet of this period, *Des suites de la contre-révolution de 1660 en Angleterre*, appeared a year later, in 1798.

Constant was to republish it in 1818–19 under the title, *Essai sur la contre-révolution d'Angleterre.* This version contained certain modifications appropriate to prevailing official views under the Restoration. The 1798 version was strongly republican in tone and very much in keeping with *Des réactions politiques.* It was in part a reply to a work by Boulay favoring the English Restoration and ignoring its consequences. Constant, on the contrary, uses historical precedent to argue that the consequences of a counterrevolution in France would be more horrific than anything witnessed under the Terror. Once again he vigorously defends republicanism and makes a frightening spectre out of the possibility of a return to monarchical rule.

VII   *From Directory to Consulate*

During the writing of the three main pamphlets mentioned in the last section, Constant was also associated with the various political changes which eventually resulted in Napoleon Bonaparte's election as First Consul for life in 1802. This date, as we shall see, also marked the end of the first main phase of Constant's political career. He retired from active politics for an eleven-year period, gradually returning to the political stage from 1813 onward.

In 1797, following the founding of a royalist club in the Rue de Clichy, Constant and a number of his friends grew increasingly conscious of the need for a club which would be republican in inspiration, supporting the policies of the Directory. A "Cercle Constitutionnel" was therefore founded, with Constant as its secretary, and meetings were first held in the Hôtel de Salm. Barras, one of the five Directors, was more or less patron of the group which also included Sieyès and Talleyrand. It was middle-class, republican, anticlerical and anti-Jacobin, accurately reflecting the Directory itself. At the same time, Constant frequented the *idéologue* group centered round the journal, *La Décade*, and which included Destutt de Tracy, Cabanis, Daunou, and the widow of Helvétius. In their ideas, they represented the philosophical basis of the Directory.

Nevertheless, the Directory itself was changing. The elections of May, 1797, had returned a counterrevolutionary majority, and some of Constant's worst fears seemed in danger of being realized. Two of the most republican-minded Directors, eventually joined by Barras, therefore engineered the *coup d'état* of 18 Fructidor (4 September) with the help of the army. As a result, the remaining two Directors were eliminated, the elections annulled, and the three successful Directors given powers to transport to French Guinea anyone accused of having joined an alleged plot against the republic. It hardly seems possible that the liberal Constant would condone these actions, but in fact he did so. In a speech delivered to the Cercle Constitutionnel on 16 September [24] he presented 18 Fructidor as a great liberation, while admittedly expressing some concern and unease about the deportations which followed.

Ironically, however, the destruction of the very republic which Constant valued so highly was now being prepared. The *coup d'état* of 18 Fructidor prepared in some measure for the events of 18 Brumaire (10 November 1799), which laid the foundations of Bonaparte's personal rule. By this time Sieyès, Constant's associate of the Cercle Constitutionnel, had become a Director and was intriguing with Talleyrand and Napoleon's brother Lucien for the overthrow of the Directory. A confrontation finally took place between the *Conseil des 500* and Napoleon. The latter temporarily lost his head, but the situation was eventually saved by Lucien, the army advanced, and the resistance of the *Conseil des 500* collapsed. The regime known as the Consulate was thus ushered in by military means and the government was taken over by three Consuls, of whom Napoleon was the one who really counted. The foundations were laid for a military dictatorship and although Constant later described these events as amounting to "the collapse for fourteen years of representative institutions," he began by seeking office under the Consulate and to that extent accepting the consequences of 18 Brumaire. He was by no means alone in this attitude. A number of the *idéologues* genuinely believed that Bonaparte would guarantee liberty, ensure the sovereignty of the people, and preserve constitutionalism.

The new constitution—the so-called Constitution of Year III—was in fact distinctly undemocratic. The role of popular suffrage was reduced to a minimum in the four new assemblies. Members of the Senate, nominated by the three Consuls, held office for life; the Legislative Body was nominated by the Senate from a list of deputies elected by the *départements*; the Tribunate was also nominated by the Senate, from a "national list" elected by the taxpayers; the Council of State was nominated by the First Consul. On the last day of 1799, Constant finally took public political office in France by being appointed a member of the Tribunate. This assembly of one hundred members could discuss legislative proposals, but could not amend them. It was free to express opinions, but the government was under no obligation to listen. It was a body in which Constant's tendency toward political opportunism was soon to conflict with his genuine and deeply felt liberalism.

Constant's first speech,[25] delivered on 5 January 1800, was a clear and precise rejection of the government's proposal that discussion in the Tribunate should be subject to a rigid time limit. He argued that the Council of State, by this proposal, was creating in the Tribunate the spirit of opposition which it feared. It was thus bringing about the very situation which its proposal was calculated to avoid. Despite Constant's sharply intelligent analysis, the time limit proposal was passed in the Tribunate by a comfortable majority. Nevertheless, Napoleon was angered by these signs of opposition and Constant was reproved in *Le Moniteur* for irresponsible self-advertisement. Thus began his brief, unhappy role as "opposition spokesman" in the Tribunate.

Constant delivered another striking speech on 25 January 1801 [26] in which he criticized the proposal to set up semimilitary tribunals, without a jury and with no right of appeal, to try opponents of the regime. Apart from a detailed analysis of the bill, Constant made his general position clear in the following passage:

It is easy to claim that those who reject this bill are taking sides with brigands, opposing the reestablishment of order and public safety, and hindering the necessary working of summary justice against the enemies of society.

Thus, fellow-tribunes, I would not have addressed this house had I not made it a rule never to allow myself to be influenced by considerations of this nature: once we give in, it is impossible to foresee where they will lead and to what a deplorable extent the fear of unfair interpretation can undermine our conscience and divert us from our duty.[27]

This attitude, implying that we must not be afraid to consider seriously the convictions of our opponents, granting them the rights we demand for ourselves, was extremely unpalatable to Napoleon. He is reported to have referred disparagingly to Constant and his associates as "metaphysicians" and "vermin" in his clothes. He promised to "shake them off," and before the end of January, 1802, Constant and twenty other opposition-minded tribunes had been forcibly retired.

CHAPTER 3

Empire and Monarchy

DISMISSAL from the Tribunate, together with Napoleon Bonaparte's increasing power, effectively ended those dreams of a scintillating political career which Constant had shared with Mme de Staël. At first he showed signs of considerable physical and mental exhaustion and one side of him welcomed the relative calm and quiet resulting from this political setback. Gradually, his various intellectual interests reasserted themselves and, in particular, he turned again to his ambitious study of religion as well as to political theory. There are references to these activities in the *Journaux intimes* from 1804 onward. The renewal of his love affair with Charlotte von Hardenberg also dates from 1804. For some time his private life was dominated by his passion for Charlotte, whom he married secretly in 1808, and his attempts to escape the tyranny of Mme de Staël, with whom he finally broke in 1811. Much of his turbulent personal drama found its way into his two autobiographical novels: *Adolphe*, begun in 1806, and *Cécile* which he probably began writing in 1811.

I *Understanding Events*

Where political matters are concerned, Constant used this period of retirement from public events in order to try to understand them better. He had, after all, witnessed at close quarters an amazing series of transformations during which the revolutionary and republican experiment of 1789, together with the high hopes of the Enlightenment, appeared to have led inexorably to military dictatorship and the authoritarianism of the Empire (Napoleon was Emperor of France from 1804 to 1814). Some evidence of his political thinking at this time is to be found in the so-called "Oeuvres manuscrites de 1810," seven bound volumes of manuscript which the Bibliothèque Nationale in Paris obtained in 1961. Apart from the 1810 manuscript of *Adolphe*, the most interesting of these writings are all political.

There is, for example, a translation of William Godwin's *An Enquiry concerning Political Justice and its Influence on General Virtue and Happiness* (1793), followed by a study of the author. Among English writers who opposed Edmund Burke's ideas and expressed enthusiasm for the ideals of the French revolutionaries, the name of Godwin is one of the most important along with that of Thomas Paine. It has been said of Godwin that he represents "the extreme length to which intellectualism, in its application to social and moral problems, ever went in England." [1] In fact, his search for social truth and political justice led him to something closely approaching anarchism— the inevitable result, perhaps, of an insistence both on individual freedom and certain collectivist ideals. The *Enquiry concerning Political Justice* was stimulating reading for anyone inspired by republican and revolutionary fervor. One can see how it must have interested Constant, particularly in the passages on individual freedom, even though Godwin's anarchist tendencies could not have won his unqualified approval.

The "Oeuvres manuscrites de 1810" also contain very substantial "Fragments d'un ouvrage abandonné sur la possibilité d'une Constitution républicaine dans un grand pays." In this work, more coherent than the term "Fragments" would suggest, Constant takes up in considerable detail an issue which he had already touched upon—the compatibility of republicanism with national greatness—in Chapter 6 of *De la force du gouvernement actuel*. Constant defends his identification of republicanism with national prestige on the assumption of genuine elections regularly renewed. He presumably matched theory with practice, and abandoned the work or at least renounced publication, when France entered a period of personal rule and government by plebiscite and decree.

The other main manuscript of 1810 is entitled "Principes de politique applicables à tous les gouvernements." This is again a substantial piece of writing, amounting to more than 650 pages of handwritten text. It is, of course, an earlier version of the work eventually published in May, 1815, as *Principes de politique applicables à tous les gouvernements représentatifs*. The published version contains the essence of the "Fragments" as well as the "Principes" and will be studied later in this chapter. For the moment, it is worth pointing out that the 1810 manuscript makes clear Constant's desire to discover and understand political fundamentals. In one of the opening pages we read: "Political principles exist independently of all forms of constitution and it still seems useful that they should be developed. Because they apply to all types of government . . . and are equally compatible with a monarchy or a republic, whatever the forms these latter take, principles can be discussed frankly and confidently." [2] The task of developing political principles and discussing them in detail thus occupied much of Constant's time during his enforced retirement from active participation in politics. In some ways it was a theoretical preparation for his return to public life which began, tentatively at first, in 1813.

II *Contacts with Bernadotte*

Following his break with Mme de Staël in 1811, Constant spent the next two years with his wife, Charlotte, in Germany and particularly in Göttingen. Here he continued working on his study of religion and mixed with a German intellectual élite of philosophers, theologians, historians, and philologists. Nevertheless, he sometimes longed for the earlier excitements of public life, was often bored by Charlotte, and thoughts of Mme de Staël —less formidable and more stimulating now that he had escaped from her immediate domination—occurred from time to time. Consequently, when she wrote to him from Sweden in November, 1812, in part chiding him for his political inactivity, particularly on the subject of Prince Bernadotte, her letter found a positive response.

Charles Bernadotte, Prince of Ponte-Corvo and a former Marshal of France, had become heir to the Swedish throne in 1810. For some time Mme de Staël had considered him a possible successor to Napoleon as Emperor of France and as a desirable alternative to a restored Bourbon monarchy. He had also received some encouragement from the Russian Tsar, Alexander I, and Mme de Staël now suggested that Constant should actively promote his cause. In fact, Constant hesitated for some time. He had been considering a move to England, but active and effective support of Bernadotte would make this undesirable or impossible. On the other hand, various relatives and friends of

Constant were already backing Bernadotte and he was influenced by their attitude. By 17 April 1813 Mme de Staël was writing, in exasperation and with some justification, that Benjamin lacked decisiveness. His *Journal intime* of the previous month contains the significant entry: "Nothing achieved. In my inmost being I feel a bitter pain at the disarray of my life. The decisive moment has come. Busy and honorable career, or complete rest, or death. This summer will decide . . ."[3] Nevertheless, by October, Constant had still not reached a decision and continued to note in his *Journal* that the moment of decision had arrived. He sensed that to build a political future on the ground provided by Bernadotte's cautious ambition was to build on shifting sand. In the meantime, he had begun a verse epic which —at least in its final form—was not wholly anti-Napoleonic in tone. Against an imaginary sixth-century background, Napoleon appeared as Argaléon and Bernadotte figured under the name of Ericus, rex Scandinaviae. The poetry, as such, was execrable and the political value of the epic nonexistent.

Mme de Staël continued to write, assuring Constant of Bernadotte's regard for him and describing the latter's political views as being in close agreement with those of herself and Benjamin. Eventually, Constant and Bernadotte met in Hanover and had eight interviews between 6 and 14 November. Their subsequent letters[4] make it clear that Constant took much of the initiative. They cast some doubt on the traditional view that Bernadotte originally asked Constant to write a political pamphlet on his behalf. By now Constant was personally committed to Bernadotte, though he still doubted the political wisdom of this move. Indeed, he was convinced—rightly as it turned out— that although Bernadotte had designs on the French throne, he would not risk losing the Swedish succession.

The anti-Napoleonic movement centered around Prince Bernadotte reached a climax when he entered Paris a week after Napoleon signed his own abdication on 6 April 1814. It disintegrated almost immediately, however, with Bernadotte's return to Stockholm where, four years later, he ascended the Swedish throne as Charles XIV.

III *Opposing Napoleon*

Nevertheless, the Bernadotte episode was not without its advantages for Constant, particularly since it led directly to the writing of one of his major political pamphlets, *De l'esprit de conquête et de l'usurpation dans leurs rapports avec la civilisation européenne.* He began writing late in November and the work appeared on 30 January 1814. Prior to this he had written some short pamphlets and articles and one of them in particular, "Mémoire sur les communications à établir avec l'intérieur de la France," [5] anticipated ideas developed at length later.

Starting from the assumption that neither freedom nor lasting peace is possible while Napoleon rules France, the "Mémoire" advocates the driving of what was in effect a propaganda wedge between the Emperor and the French people. This can be done by official declarations or unofficial pamphlets. While the former method is probably the most effective in theory, the European powers are unlikely to issue the kind of anti-Napoleonic declaration Constant has in mind. Alternatively, a flow of unofficial anti-Napoleonic writings into France can be organized and controlled from Switzerland. These writings must emphasize two things: (1) Napoleon is the real enemy of France; (2) France requires above all free and representative constitutional government. The "Mémoire" was, of course, a very minor work in its scope and effect. On the other hand, *De l'esprit de conquête* proved to be a masterpiece in its own right as well as a major anti-Napoleonic document.

The speed with which *De l'esprit de conquête* was completed is explained, in part, by the fact that it contains some of the substance, and sometimes the actual text, of the manuscript "Principes" of 1810. It occupies over a hundred pages in the Pléiade edition, about one third being devoted to "l'esprit de conquête" and the remainder to "l'usurpation." A decade earlier, Constant had described himself as able to keep silent under despotism though unable to reconcile himself to it.[6] Now, in the preface to his new work, he expresses his determination to break a national conspiracy of silence, born of fear, which has earned the astonished censure of other European countries. He asserts that, were they free, virtually all Frenchmen would hasten to put their signatures to his views.

Part One, on conquest, is largely an analysis of the phenomenon of war and militarism in fifteen short chapters. It is Constant's central argument that war has become outmoded. While he recognizes the necessities, and even the virtues, of warfare at an earlier and simpler stage in human history, he believes that militarism is now out of tune with an age dominated by commerce, utility, and the desire for peace in which to pursue them. Commerce has replaced war as a means of obtaining what one wants. "War is thus prior in time to commerce. The one is savage impulse, the other civilized calculation." [7] The material and spiritual costs of modern warfare far outweigh the gains it brings. For the individual soldier, too, a genuine challenge has been replaced by an ineluctable fatality. As a result, the modern ruler who inspires in his people military aggression and a narrow, hostile patriotism is at best anachronistic and at worst vicious. He is particularly vicious because, since no European state is naturally bellicose, he must corrupt the nation systematically in order to create an effective military machine. Such a machine also demands the discipline of uniformity which means, for an ardent individualist like Constant, the dead hand of systematization, petty laws and regulations, a state bureaucracy. Constant invokes the support of both Montesquieu (*De l'Esprit des lois*) and Mirabeau (*L'Ami des hommes*) as he declares: "Variety is an organism; uniformity a mechanism. Variety is life; uniformity is death." [8] The cult of uniformity, and a generally soulless levelling process, arouse his scorn and prompt the ironical comment: "Above everything else, the great word nowadays is uniformity. It is a pity that all towns cannot be pulled down to be rebuilt on an identical plan; that mountains cannot be leveled so that the ground is consistently flat. And I am astonished that all inhabitants have not been ordered to wear the same clothes so that the master may no longer encounter any irregular medley of colors or any shocking variety." [9] This first part ends with a passionate denunciation of Napoleon ("Man of another world, cease robbing this one") though the Emperor is never actually named.

Part Two, on usurpation, deals with the arbitrary, illegitimate seizure of power and its consequences for freedom. Constant begins by saying that he has no intention of comparing "regular" or "legitimate" forms of government with one another. He accepts monarchies and republics alike, though his sympathies still lie primarily with the latter, and he contrasts the virtues of both with the vices of a usurping regime. The example of constitutional monarchy in England had impressed Constant in a number of ways and lessened his theoretical objections to royalism. Thus he is able to claim that kings at least have an appropriate training and background for high office whereas the usurper, virtually by definition, achieves and retains power only through violence and deceit. Constant goes so far as to find usurpation worse, in some ways, than despotism. Both forms of government kill liberty, but usurpation requires the outward forms of public support and therefore, having suppressed genuine freedom, it further imposes on the people a false appearance of acquiescence and a parody of liberty.

Having argued that usurpation is as much an anachronism as military aggression, Constant has to interpret Napoleon's seizure of power in France as an accidental consequence of the Revolution. Among other things, the excesses of the Revolution created an exceptional and temporary desire for strong, absolutist control. At this point, Constant goes on to discuss liberty at some length, beginning with a distinction between conceptions of liberty in the ancient and modern worlds. The small scale of the Greek city state enabled the individual citizen (though not the slave majority) to participate directly in public affairs. In large modern states this is not possible; participation is indirect, through elections. We have already seen (in Chapter 1) that Constant goes on to show that the men of 1789, influenced particularly by Rousseau and Mably, wrongly tried to secure the freedom of the Greek *polis* in a modern state— wrongly, because it could only be done by force and because they identified freedom with a tyrannical egalitarianism. As a consequence, the pursuit of liberty resulted in its suppression. It is not surprising that so many citizens became horrified by the term "liberty," since it had thus become identified closely (though mistakenly) with tyranny. In order to escape mass tyranny, therefore, the bulk of the nation yielded (again mistakenly) to a single tyrant. The power which he enjoyed, even had he been *per impossible* a virtuous and moderate man, was bound to corrupt him. It is impossible for a tyrant to govern with moderation and retain his power. The usurper must continually take measures to secure the basic illegitimacy of his position.

The later chapters of Part Two inevitably concentrate on a subject which we have already seen recurring in Constant's political writings—arbitrary power and arbitrary government. Here he demonstrates their destructive effect on intellectual progress, freedom of the press, the judicial system, true religion, and even family life. Not least of all, the arts and sciences deteriorate markedly when tied to the service of the state.

In the final chapter, Constant expresses his confidence that usurpation is doomed to failure and defeat. He is encouraged by the historical example of England. During the English Civil War of the seventeenth century, many inhuman excesses occurred and afterward the country appeared to have lapsed into servitude, like France. Nevertheless, he sees England as having become a model for other countries and a source of hope; it has taken its place among the wise, virtuous, and free nations of the world, and France will soon do the same.

De l'esprit de conquête et de l'usurpation, which Constant called his "anti-Napoleonic enterprise," was generally well received, particularly by those with right-wing sympathies. Mme de Staël on the other hand, after an initially favorable reaction, expressed some reservations on the subject of Benjamin's lack of patriotism. Constant wrote to various friends to reassure them that he saw the overthrow of Napoleon as a first step only. He would be anxious to eliminate subsequently the possibility of any purely reactionary successor. Thus he wrote (in English) to the old friend of his Edinburgh days, by that time become Sir James Mackintosh: "He [Napoleon] must fall before we can think of anything else; he must fall, that we may have time to think of anything else. I am sometimes vexed, but never frightened, at the attempts other governments, even while they struggle against him, are making to establish their own despotism. Let us pull down the master, and easy will it be to check those awkward apprentices." [10]

Finally, as we have already seen, there is a sense in which this pamphlet was designed to help Bernadotte as well as to discomfort Napoleon. The two men are contrasted—markedly to Bernadotte's advantage, though neither is named—in the second chapter of Part Two.[11] In Chapter 5 of the first edition (a chapter subsequently suppressed), there is another passage supporting Bernadotte by implication and pointing to the virtues shared by the English monarchy of 1688 and the Swedish of 1810.[12] In these circumstances it is not surprising that Bernadotte should have praised the pamphlet without reservation in a letter of 3 February 1814,[13] also announcing the award to Constant of the Order of the Polar Star.

IV *The Virtues of Royalty*

With the failure of Bernadotte's ambitions, Constant began at once to minimize his own part in the affair. As regards the man himself, however, he retained a considerable personal regard for Bernadotte. It seems clear that his renewed political activities of 1813 and 1814 had contained the usual mixture of opportunism and idealism, two elements that were to be combined in a more puzzling and curious way a year later.

For the moment, the important facts were that Napoleon had signed a declaration of intention to abdicate on 4 April 1814, and two days later the first Bourbon Restoration began with the proclamation of Louis XVIII as King. He was soon to enter Paris, on 3 May, among scenes of great enthusiasm. Constant was not *persona grata* either with the deposed Napoleon or with the legitimist supporters of Louis XVIII. Nevertheless, he had already moved significantly in the direction of monarchism. There had been clear signs in *De l'esprit de conquête* that he was prepared to tolerate a form of royalty—a king who would be subject to constitutional control and who would govern through ministers working within an agreed framework of law. These ideas were elaborated further in two relatively short pamphlets published in May and August: *Réflexions sur les constitutions, la distribution des pouvoirs et les garanties dans une monarchie constitutionnelle* and *Observations sur le discours de S. E. le Ministre de l'Intérieur en faveur du projet de loi sur la liberté de la presse.* He advocated the political neutrality of the crown, an hereditary peerage, religious toleration, press freedom, and trial by jury. In fact, most of these provisions had been included in the Charter of 1814, drawn up by the King's advisers, though the King still embodied the legislative power. The Charter also declared the inviolability of all property confiscated during the Revolution (i.e., the *émigrés* and the clergy lost a substantial amount of land for good), and provision was made for parliamentary control of taxation.

At the end of August, Constant fell suddenly in love with Mme Récamier. The affair lasted for more than twelve months. He had known her for a number of years, had once wittily and maliciously described her as enjoying "neither the repose of virtue nor the delights of transgression," but was now completely infatuated. The fact that she was an ardent royalist encouraged his new political tendencies. He even wrote to her: "Take possession of my faculties; profit by my devotion to you to benefit your country and enhance my fame." The way seemed reasonably clear for eventual political recognition by the new constitutional monarchy when Constant's whole future—even his personal safety—was put in doubt by the dramatic news, on 5 March 1815, that Napoleon had escaped from Elba and landed in the south of France.

V The Hundred Days

One may admire Constant's courage in remaining in France after the news of Napoleon's return. In the circumstances, his attacks on the "usurper" now took on a distinctly dangerous character. To add to his difficulties, he had been regarded with suspicion and dislike by the restored French court. Nevertheless, partly through the influence of his continuing infatuation for Mme Récamier, he now pushed courage to the pitch of recklessness when, on 19 March, he published in the *Journal des débats* a notoriously outspoken diatribe against Napoleon. It included the famous passage: "Napoleon has not promised clemency. . . . He is Attila, he is Genghis Khan, but more terrible and more odious because the resources of civilization are his to use. I have sought liberty in all its forms; I have seen that it is only possible under the monarchy; I have seen the king ally himself with the nation. I shall not go, a miserable renegade, dragging myself from one source of power to another, concealing infamy with sophistry and stammering profaned words in order to redeem a shameful life." [14] The following day Napoleon entered Paris and Louis XVIII was already in flight to Ghent.

There now occurred what has generally been regarded as the most discreditable phase of Constant's political career. A month after the *Journal des débats* article, he had become a Counsellor of State to "Genghis Khan." He first went into hiding outside Paris, learnt that his name did not figure on the list of exceptions to the general amnesty proclaimed by Napoleon, eventually returned to Paris (28 March), and gave Sébastiani, who had deserted the Bourbons for Napoleon, a letter to be shown to the authorities. We do not know the contents of this letter but, probably as a result, Constant had satisfactory meetings with both Fouché and Joseph Bonaparte. On 14 April he had his first interview with the Emperor—to be followed by half-a-dozen more during the remainder of the month. On 19 April his nomination to the Council of State had been announced, to the fury of the royalists and the consternation of his friends and relatives.

It would seem that Napoleon had now decided on a more liberal policy, appropriate to the changed social and political circumstances, and wanted to hear Constant's advice. In the *Mémoires sur les Cent Jours* (*Memoirs of the Hundred Days*), written about five years later, Constant claims that he did not believe for a moment in the Emperor's "sudden conversion." There are elements of special pleading and rationalization here, and indeed the *Journal* entries for the second half of April display a more convincing and characteristic mixture of caution, admiration, criticism, recklessness and self-seeking in his attitude to Napoleon. The advice to which the latter was willing to listen, but which he was not necessarily prepared to accept, was on the subject of constitutional change. On 24 April the *Moniteur* published the "Acte additionnel aux Constitutions de l'Empire." Constant was one of the main authors, and the Act became popularly known as "la Benjamine." The authors did not have things all their own way, however, and Napoleon resisted a number of Constant's suggestions. Still, the new constitution testified to his consistency, at least on the level of political theory, and was a somewhat improved version of Louis XVIII's "Charte." Constant's own criticisms of it are chiefly found in the *Principes de politique applicables à tous les gouvernements représentatifs* which he was preparing for publication at this time. For example, in Chapter 5, he emphasizes the desirability of direct voting rather than an electoral college system.

As things turned out, the "Benjamine" aroused little enthusiasm, despite the resurgence of popular support for Napoleon. The disaster of Waterloo followed soon afterward. As for

Constant, his activities during the Hundred Days led to accusations of the most shameful apostasy. The essence of his defense, based on patriotic practicality, was to reply: "I have been reproached, in a lampoon, for not having had myself killed beside the throne which I defended on 19 March. In fact, on 20 March, I looked up and saw that the throne had disappeared but that France remained." [15]

This passage comes from the *Mémoires sur les Cent Jours* in which Constant later excused himself with considerable eloquence and ingenuity. He argued that he had acted not out of self-interest, but from a desire to save France from foreign invasion and civil war. Furthermore, he had helped to force Napoleon to accept a liberal constitution and had thereby ensured a democratic check on his despotic tendencies. As for Napoleon's popular reception in France, Constant interprets this as a natural reaction to the views and plans of many of the royalist extremists who had flocked back to the court of Louis XVIII. He argues that the "Charte" was already being perverted and exploited for reactionary purposes.

Earlier in the *Mémoires* (Part 2, letter 4), Constant had also analyzed the shortcomings of the "Acte additionnel." This may serve to remind us that the whole tone of the *Mémoires* is not only related to 1815, but colored by 1820 and the second Restoration. Constant asserts with some passion that his support of Louis XVIII before and after 1815 is not in contradiction with his cooperation with Napoleon. On Napoleon's return, constitutional monarchy ("the best form of government") disappeared. But with foreign powers threatening the nation's territorial integrity, the Emperor became necessary for the preservation of a France subsequently to be governed by an enlightened king. And in a final postscript, Constant quotes from his *De l'esprit de conquête* to demonstrate his consistency and reassert his conviction that governments, to be legitimate, must be called to power either by free elections or by a widely accepted hereditary principle. The former seems the more attractive in theory, but in fact it has often been counterfeited.

Constant makes a good case, though not always a convincing one. The late Harold Nicolson was right to insist that he was not simply a run-of-the-mill opportunist.[16] The element of hindsight in the *Mémoires* should not blind us to the foresight which

Constant displayed in 1815, with his (justified) fears of another White Terror and his general reading of contemporary events. But as we saw in Chapter 1, he was a complex and contradictory person. His actions during the Hundred Days were a characteristic amalgam of private ambition, gambling instincts, considerable political insight, and genuine patriotism.

VI *Political Fundamentals*

We referred earlier in this chapter to the *Principes de politique applicables à tous les gouvernements représentatifs* which Constant published little more than a fortnight before Waterloo and which contains material from earlier writings which had remained in manuscript in 1810. It is certainly one of his half dozen major political pamphlets—and for many critics the most important of them. Although expressing attitudes and arguments with which we are already familiar, it is of particular interest since it includes Constant's careful reflexions on a number of fundamental political and constitutional issues. In the preface, he himself refers to the element of repetition and cites this as evidence of consistency on his part. He also attributes a distinctive power of conviction to his pamphlet, taking the Enlightenment view that "there exists in the human mind a natural reason which always ends by accepting the evidence . . ."

The first chapter, on the sovereignty of the people, shows a new sophistication in Constant's thought—a sophistication which is clearly the fruit of twenty years of very varied political experience. He begins from the theoretical position that the general will can find expression in any form of government, depending on the time and the circumstances. A government, therefore, which genuinely reflects the will of the people, is legitimate; only government by force, against the people's will, is illegitimate and inadmissible. At the same time, experience had made it clear to Constant—the use of plebiscites during the Empire would be an example—that the general will can be falsely and misleadingly invoked. In addition, the sovereignty of the people must be subject to limitations. To make it limitless is to give the leaders of the people a dangerous excess of power. History has shown, repeatedly, that certain decisions or actions must be rejected or resisted even if it is claimed that they emanate from the general will. Indeed, no one section of the community has a right to completely unlimited powers. Above all, individual freedom must always take precedence over the sovereignty of the people.

This is no doubt a typical expression of early nineteenth-century liberalism—more satisfactory in theory than in practice. At no point, for example, does Constant face the problem of the individual freedom of political usurpers or counterrevolutionaries and its relation to the general will. Must their freedom take precedence over the sovereignity of the people? He seems to be caught in the old liberal dilemma—how to reconcile private freedom and public justice.

Moving on to more directly constitutional matters, Constant sketches the role of the king in a constitutional monarchy. He emphasizes the distinctive functions and authority to be given to ministers, insists (with the example of England in mind) on the separation of the executive, legislative and judicial functions, and sees royal neutrality as ideally suited to ensuring the satisfactory operation of all three. This royal role also makes clear the fundamental difference between a constitutional and an absolute monarchy—and the constitutional superiority of the former. On these, and related, grounds Constant also finds constitutional monarchy superior to a republican form of government. He outlines the disadvantages of republican constitutions in a way that again emphasizes his increasingly moderate liberalism and which contrasts sharply with the ideas which he had reiterated between 1794 and 1802.

In his comments on the legislature, Constant had expressed his approval of a two-chamber system, an hereditary chamber and one elected by popular vote. He takes the idea of the hereditary chamber seriously enough to devote a further chapter to it. He sees it as a desirable intermediary between the monarch and the elected representatives of the people. Furthermore, he argues that it is important to set the peers to work and not create the type of idle, privileged nobility which was a factor in the revolutionary upsurge of 1789. Finally, he considers it important to create further peers among men of outstanding ability. Once more invoking the example of England, he writes: "We find the hereditary peerage in Great Britain compatible with a high degree of civil and political liberty; all distinguished citizens can attain to the peerage. It does not have the one odious feature of the hereditary system—exclusiveness. The day after an ordinary citizen's nomination he enjoys the same legal privileges as the most long-standing peer." [17]

As regards the elected representatives sitting in the second chamber, they must be chosen by direct vote and not, as in the "Acte additionnel," by electoral colleges from selected lists. Once more he points to the British model: "If we in France wish to enjoy for once the full benefits of representative government, we must have direct elections. Since 1788 such elections have brought to the British House of Commons all well-educated men. One would have difficulty in mentioning an Englishman, distinguished for his political gifts, who has not been successful if he sought election." [18]

This last point leads on to the question of property, especially landed property. Constant's rather simplistic (and paternalistic) argument runs as follows: to possess landed property is to have leisure; to have leisure allows a man to achieve an understanding of public affairs; therefore owners of landed property are uniquely fitted to sit in parliament and contribute to the debates and decisions of the legislative power. In short, all citizens have civil rights, but only those who possess landed property have political privileges.

In the course of this argument—and conscious, perhaps, of its illiberal character—Constant distinguishes in a lapidary phrase between patriotism which gives one the courage to die for one's country and patriotism which enables one to recognize its best interests. The first kind of patriotism, particularly useful in time of war, he attributes to the common people; the second is the type of patriotism which should activate the nation's legislators.

While still on the subject of property, Constant shows little sympathy with the claims of industrialists or members of the liberal professions to represent the people. Where industrialists in particular are concerned, he asserts that industrial property simply assures the independence of individuals, whereas landed property guarantees the stability of institutions. Hence, in his view, the superior claims of the latter.

In a later chapter (Chapter 15), Constant returns to the question of property, insisting on its inviolability and expressing his complete opposition to the confiscation of private property by the state. Indeed, he regards the individual's right to own property as an essential, and fundamentally important, freedom. (Twenty-one years later, Proudhon was to argue the opposite view and describe private property as a form of theft.) At the same time, Constant did go so far as to say that property is "a social convention" in the sense that it only exists significantly in and through society. On these grounds Laboulaye, thirty years after Constant's death, described his views as dangerously close to a theoretical justification of communism.[19] In fact, however, Constant held that only the complete elimination of manual work (through the invention of increasingly sophisticated machinery) would make the abolition of private property possible. In 1815 he did not regard this prospect as belonging to the foreseeable future. He also wrote: "The abolition of private property would destroy the division of labor—the basis of improvement in all the arts and sciences. The capacity for progress, which is the favorite hope of the writers whom I oppose, would perish owing to lack of time and independence. The crude and forcibly imposed equality which they advocate would form an invincible obstacle to the gradual establishment of true equality—equality based on happiness and understanding."[20]

Later, Constant returns to the question of state interference and the financing of the national debt either through taxes or loans. He quotes from Necker, J.-B. Say, and Adam Smith. He severely criticizes the tendency of governments to fail to honor their debts while declaring individuals bankrupt, or imprisoning them for not meeting their financial obligations. He also attacks governments for misusing the taxes they impose on individuals by spending them on war rather than peace. Not least, he takes the unexceptionable view that taxation is in any case an evil, if a necessary one, which must be kept to an absolute minimum.

The final chapters of the *Principes* mainly deal with various desirable manifestations of freedom—freedom of the press, religious freedom, individual freedom, and the independence of the judiciary. These are matters which Constant wrote about repeatedly and they will be discussed separately in the next chapter.

VII *Entry into Parliament*

The last fourteen years of Constant's life, coterminous with the second Bourbon Restoration (1816–30), also represent the most practically active phase of his political career. He eventually became a deputy in 1819 and, apart from one break of sixteen months, represented either the Sarthe, Paris, or Alsace until his death. He became an outstanding parliamentarian and during this time, as has been rightly said, he taught his fellow countrymen the nature and processes of parliamentary democracy.[21]

With the defeat of Waterloo and the restoration of Louis XVIII, Constant's political career began very inauspiciously. Initially, his name figured on the royalist list of proscribed persons but was eventually removed by the King himself as the result of an *apologia* (something like a first draft of the *Mémoires sur les Cent Jours*) which Constant sent him. In 1816 Constent spent some months in England, partly as a precautionary measure. He attended the House of Commons and generally profited from the occasion to study and admire the functioning of British parliamentary democracy at first hand. During this period *Adolphe* was published in London and Paris and eventually, on 16 September, Constant and his wife returned to the French capital.

It was also in September that the repressive first government of Louis XVIII was replaced by a more balanced Chamber of Deputies. Under the new arrangements, the main opposition party, the "Doctrinaires," was essentially a centrist group. It included such men as Royer-Collard, Prosper de Barante, the young Guizot, and Charles de Rémusat. Constant sympathized with some of the Doctrinaires' ideas, but he soon moved toward the left-wing liberals. With his past record, there was no possibility of ministerial office under the Bourbons, and Constant's role, when he eventually entered parliament, was that of opposition watchdog. The liberals' aim to "royalize the nation and nationalize the monarchy" was very much in keeping with his own ideas, but even where the liberals were concerned he took up a position distinctly to the left in many matters. Eventually, he even modified his ideas about landed property. He became an essentially independent deputy who frequently made common cause with the liberals.

In December, 1816, Constant had published *De la doctrine qui peut réunir les partis en France*. He won favor by his attempt to point the way to a reconciliation between the *émigrés* and the better features of the revolutionary tradition. During 1817 he published various further pamphlets and wrote in the *Mercure de France*. The press laws governing periodicals such as the *Mercure* made free expression difficult, however, and in January, 1818, the editors, with the help of various collaborators including Constant, launched *La Minerve française* in the form of four volumes published at irregular intervals during the year. Constant contributed articles and book reviews. The *Minerve* lasted for two and a half years and was the semiofficial organ of the liberal opposition. It was also in 1818 that there began to appear the four volumes of Constant's *Collection complète des ouvrages publiés sur le gouvernement représentatif et la constitution actuelle de la France, formant une espèce de Cours de politique constitutionnelle* (*Collected Works on Representative Government*).

In the summer of 1818, Constant fell and as a result had to use crutches for the rest of his life. In the following October he failed to be elected to the Chamber of Deputies, but was returned as representative for the *département* of the Sarthe in March, 1819. Despite some unprepossessing physical characteristics, he became in time a very successful and influential parliamentary orator. Recalling his achievements as a public speaker, L.-M. Cormenin wrote in 1842:

He had a slender body, thin legs, a stooping posture and long arms. His fair curly hair fell on to his shoulders, pleasantly framing his expressive features. His teeth got in the way of his tongue and produced a feminine manner of speaking, lisping and rather mumbling. When he read from a text his voice had a monotonous drawl. When he improvised, he leaned with both hands on the marble of the rostrum and a flow of words gushed forth. Nature had denied him the external advantages of bearing, gesture and voice . . . but he made up for this by intellectual power and hard work . . .

He had such powers of concentration and composed with such facility that, while listening to a political opponent, he was able to write a refutation which he then read immediately at the rostrum. And nothing was lacking in terms of method, construction, argument and style.[22]

Cormenin adds that Constant, like other liberal orators of the day, did not always impress his fellow deputies, though his speeches enjoyed great influence among the extraparliamentary public. While his contributions to debates did not immediately affect much legislation, they formed and educated a public opinion in the light of which later laws were framed and earlier laws modified.

If 1819 was a memorable year for Constant personally, 1820 was a dramatic year in terms of general French politics. In February, the Duc de Berry, younger son of the Comte d' Artois (the future Charles X), was assassinated as he left the Paris Opéra. The crime as such was an isolated one, but it provoked a violent royalist reaction. The right-wing Duc de Richelieu was recalled to office to lead the administration, a number of repressive laws were passed, and the "ultras" or ultraroyalists held power until 1830. An intensified policy of authoritarian rule followed the death of Louis XVIII in 1824 and the accession of Charles X (who had declared that he would rather hew wood than be a king like George IV of England). Constant was not a deputy during part of the last two years of Louis XVIII's reign, but he was reelected (for Paris) in March, 1824, six months before Charles X ascended the throne. During this time there were many features of public life which offended his liberal convictions, and he continued to be active as a political commentator and theorist.

It was in the years 1822 and 1824 respectively that the two parts of Constant's *Commentaire sur l'ouvrage de Filangieri* (*Commentary on the Works of Filangieri*) were published. Gaetano Filangieri was an Italian jurist whose *Scienza della legislazione* appeared in a series of volumes published from 1780 until his death in 1788. He wrote on a variety of subjects— legislation, education, religion, etc.—but his economic ideas in particular linked him with the Physiocrats, whose theories were influential in the second half of the eighteenth century. They advocated free trade and the sweeping away of all national customs barriers. They also believed that the land was *the* essential source of wealth. Constant claims to share Filangieri's aims but to disagree with his methods. In fact, his comments on Filangieri's ideas suggest that he had little sympathy with the Physiocrats, particularly because of their leaning toward political despotism. He was also opposed to their theories of taxation and their emphasis on agriculture to the virtual exclusion of industry. Indeed, on this last point, he had come to recognize the inevitability of social change and the fact that social structures were steadily evolving in the direction of greater equality. He did not seek to oppose this trend; to do so would have been to attempt to ignore historical inevitability. In general, Constant's economic ideas, though neither particularly distinguished nor original, were progressive in the sense that they grew to favor the rising industrial class rather than the declining landed aristocracy.

It is clear that Constant was as deeply influenced by Adam Smith and Malthus in his economic ideas as he was by Montesquieu in his political theories. In the *Commentaire sur l'ouvrage de Filangieri*, he resembles Adam Smith in seeing value as being based on labor and enhanced by the division of labor so that all social classes—landowners, industrialists, artisans, etc.—increase production and their own status by performing their distinctive economic roles in the pursuit of self-interest. In particular, they must have genuine freedom and be unhampered by state interference, monopolies, and other restrictions. For Constant, the individual is central in the economy, and he went further than Adam Smith in his advocacy of *laissez-faire* ideas. He opposed restrictions on imports and exports and argued against government limitation of wages and the rates of interest on borrowed capital.

There is little about poverty or social welfare in Constant's writings, yet Harold Nicolson was less than fair when he described Constant's intelligence as luminous but without warmth. In fact, particularly as a parliamentarian, Constant had a deserved reputation as a champion of the oppressed. Apart from his honorable role in such matters as the Regnault and Caffé affairs, he was an eloquent opponent of the slave trade, notably in speeches delivered in 1821 and 1822.[23] The same acute sense of injustice prompted him in 1825, during the Greek War of Independence, to publish an *Appel aux nations chrétiennes en faveur des Grecs*.

VIII *The Last Phase*

The final six years of Constant's political career require little comment. He had become increasingly isolated, within the Chamber, as a dogged independent. Outside parliament, however, he continued to enjoy great popularity, particularly among his Alsatian constituents (he represented Bas-Rhin from 1827 onwards) and among young people and students. By the latter he was regarded as a champion of freedom and justice.

In 1824 he successfully defeated an attempt to have his election declared invalid on the grounds that he was a foreigner. From 1824 onward, the five volumes of his lifelong work on religion began to appear. His greatest disappointment was his failure, despite his writings, to be elected to the French Academy (he had the backing of Chateaubriand).

In and out of parliament he continued to speak and write with considerable energy despite deteriorating health. He showed himself to be well informed about a wide range of foreign problems in which he took a deep interest. As regards domestic politics, the last dramatic event with which he was associated was the July Revolution of 1830.

Charles X's reign had been repressive and reactionary and things began to come to a head after 1827 when the citizen army was disbanded and a rigorous press censorship introduced. The elections which followed went against the government. The consequent Martignac ministry lasted for two years and then the King appointed Polignac, described as "the incarnation of the *ancien régime*," as Prime Minister. Significantly, too, La Bourdonnaye, identified with the White Terror of 1815, became Minister of the Interior. The Chamber was dissolved in 1830, elections were held in June and July and the increasingly strong and coherent opposition scored a crushing electoral victory over the government. On 25 July, the King issued the infamous Ordinances of Saint-Cloud which suspended press freedom, dissolved the newly elected parliament, restricted the vote to those who paid land tax, and required a new parliament to be elected on this narrow franchise. The "Three Glorious Days' —27, 28, and 29 July—followed, with the barricades going up in Paris and the city in the hands of the revolutionaries by the third day. The King then withdrew the Ordinances, but it was too late.

He was obliged to abdicate and Louis-Philippe was proclaimed King on 7 August.

At the moment when the Ordinances of Saint-Cloud were issued, Constant was convalescing in the country after a serious operation. Nevertheless, despite the advice of his doctor and the pleas of his family, he traveled to Paris, visited various barricades on 28 and 29 July, and openly advertised his support for the opponents of the regime. A couple of days later, he and Sébastiani drew up the declaration requesting Louis-Philippe, as Duc d'Orléans, to accept the duties of lieutenant-general of the realm. After a further week, Louis-Philippe became King and Constant was appointed a councillor of state and chairman of the legislative committee. Although he received a generous financial gift from the King, his highest political ambitions went unrealized, his health continued to deteriorate, and he died on 8 December from a creeping paralysis.

CHAPTER 4

Categories of Freedom

T HE extent of Constant's preoccupation with freedom has already been emphasized in the three previous chapters. The meanings which he gives to the term vary in different contexts, but we have seen that he was especially opposed to any form of undue interference by the state in social or individual life. The adjective "undue" begs several questions, of course, and Constant was not always consistent in its application. Also, he ran into difficulties, of which he often seemed unaware, on the question of reconciling individual and social liberty. In general, however, his concern with freedom put him on the side of the angels, particularly on such topics as press censorship, the slave traffic, religious intolerance, etc. Across the whole range of such questions, he worked from the basic assumption that unhampered knowledge and unfettered truth can only be sources of good. A short passage from the "Oeuvres manuscrites de 1810" puts his view uncompromisingly: "Every time one thinks there has been an abuse of knowledge there has been, in fact, a lack of knowledge. Every time one accuses truth of having produced evil, this evil has been the result not of truth but of error. To say that truth can be dangerous is to make a terrible accusation against a Providence which has placed the search for truth among the necessities of mankind." [1] With this starting point in mind, we can now look more closely at Constant's views on certain specific issues by way of a pendant, as it were, to his political ideas.

I *Freedom of the Press*

Political events, particularly during the Bourbon Restoration, made press freedom a major issue during Constant's most active and immediate participation in public affairs. With characteristic moderation, he did not demand complete license, and in the

Principes de politique (Chapter XVI) lists those issues on which the press must be firmly controlled: incitement to murder, incitement to civil war, encouragement of a foreign enemy, direct insults against the head of state. On this latter point in particular he praises British press laws and describes England as *la terre classique* of press freedom.

The general question of freedom to publish is one to which Constant returned repeatedly in pamphlets and speeches. Two of his best-known pamphlets on the subject are *De la liberté des brochures, des pamphlets et des journaux considérée sous le rapport de l'intérêt du gouvernement* and *Observations sur le discours prononcé par S. E. le Ministre de l'Intérieur en faveur du projet de loi sur la liberté de la presse*. Both were published in 1814 and both take a severely practical approach to political censorship.

It is Constant's thesis in *De la liberté des brochures* that, despite the increasing number and growing circulation of newspapers and pamphlets of all kinds, it is in the government's own interest that they should not be subject to any prior censorship. He takes this view both of publications appearing in France itself and those which find their way there from other European countries. He has in mind political, not moral, censorship and holds that any form of prior restriction would only encourage an undersirable clandestine press—undesirable because it would be more extreme and more difficult to control. It has been argued, of course, that to punish certain kinds of publication by legal sanctions only is to act after the damage has been done and the sedition printed. Constant rejects this argument for censorship prior to printing on the grounds that illicit material will appear in any case, whatever the measures taken, and make such censorship ultimately ineffectual.

Continuing this practical approach, his case against censorship amounts to saying that in a civilized and democratic society it is not a genuine possibility. Attempted censorship has its own very real attendant evils and he strongly dislikes constitutional efforts to make the censor an instrument of government policy— the more so when judges, for example, are rightly required to show complete political independence and impartiality. A series of further practical points follows. If government censorship becomes a reality, then the government is naturally identified in people's minds with everything the newspapers say. This can be highly embarrassing for any government. Alternatively, if an individual journalist has been particularly extreme or indiscreet, the government will be forced to issue a formal denial which immediately becomes suspect. Again, under censorship, any newspaper criticism—however slight—of an individual is interpreted as an official judgment of that individual. Fourthly, government apologists will leave no room, in approved publications, for an expression of views by genuinely independent-minded commentators. Finally, even without the most severe forms of censorship, opinion in France generally tends far too much to reflect opinion in Paris. Constant therefore insists on the need for greater independence of views in the provinces and believes that guarantees against a depressing uniformity of thought can only be created and secured by the existence of genuinely independent local newspapers. In a speech delivered six years later, in 1820, he made the related point that a government which imposes political censorship condemns itself to a sometimes crippling degree of ignorance by muzzling the open expression of a significant section of public opinion.

In his *Observations sur le discours prononcé par S. E. le Ministre de l'Intérieur*, Constant criticized in detail a speech by abbé de Montesquiou, Minister of the Interior, in defense of a government bill imposing censorship on all publications of less than twenty pages. Much of the pamphlet is in fact taken up with the familiar issue of what constitutes legitimate ministerial responsibility and authority under the crown. On the more direct question of censorship, Constant naturally regards the limit of twenty pages as arbitrary and illogical. As for the Minister's argument that French literature reached unparalleled heights of excellence under the tight control of Louis XIV, Constant rejects this as irrelevant. He adds tartly: "If a citizen is arbitrarily arrested, what interest is it to him, and to his family and friends, that a bill which suppresses his complaints favors the best authors?" [2] He regards as more serious than the status of classical literature the censoring of publications which contribute to the maintenance of individual freedom, independence of conscience, the administration of justice, the improvement of certain laws, and the just distribution of taxes. In any case, he says, because there was no press freedom under Louis XIV, more than a million of his subjects were banished, Protestant citizens were persecuted, and the King was singularly ill-informed about both French and European public opinion—with serious military consequences.

In a speech of 1827, Constant took a characteristically realistic view of censorship by admitting that it strongly tempts all governments, republican or royalist, because of its close link with the exercise of power. It is also in various speeches delivered between 1820 and 1827 that he comes nearest to a more sweeping moral condemnation of censorship. He argues that it eventually inhibits truth (and therefore true progress) in such fundamental sphere as knowledge, law, religion, ethics. This is a viewpoint he had indicated earlier (*De la liberté des brochures*) in a quotation from Bentham, and he returned to it in 1827. The freedom of the press is the concern of everyone since the evil of censorship eventually spreads beyond pamphlets and newspapers to all aspects of life. Censorship is an immense net which sooner or later entangles in its toils not only opinions but also facts, not only political dissent but also moral integrity.

II *Educational Independence*

The independence of mind to which a free, uncensored press appeals, and on which it feeds, leads naturally to the broad question of education. Constant did not write a great deal on the subject, but his *Commentaire sur l'ouvrage de Filangieri* contains an interesting chapter on educational freedom. As we might expect, he is opposed to state control of education. The role of the government should be to provide the facilities but not to influence objectives. For Constant, government-controlled education too often means the teaching of those facts and opinions of which a given administration happens to approve. He points out that if education were handed over to the state in this sense, sudden changes of government would mean that while one generation of schoolchildren was trained in dissent, the next might well be nurtured in the most abject conformism. Generally, political manipulation of the educational process represents a fundamental attack on individual liberty.

On these grounds, and despite his own unfortunate experience with private tutors as a young boy, Constant clearly favors private, individual tuition. He is not against government schools as such, nor against the spread of popular education (though he did oppose compulsory schooling). What he fears is that governments will be tempted to move on from state *provision* in the direction of increasing state *control*. At the same time, he was not blind to the disadvantages of the private system. Theoretically, he says, and to some degree in practice, schools controlled by the state have the advantage of grouping children in fair-sized classes so that a given individual meets and mixes with a cross-section of other children of the same age. In this way, purely academic education is enhanced by that other important form of education which consists in learning to live with one's fellow human beings. A second disadvantage of private tuition, when it exists side by side with public provision, is the fact that a government will have a strong tendency to discriminate against those who have been privately educated and only appoint to the staff of its schools the products of its own state system. This problem, and the independence of mind which Constant associates with private tuition, are both expressed in the following passage:

Governments which do not appear to interfere with private education always favor, nonetheless, the institutions which they have created. They demand of candidates for appointment to posts in the public sector a kind of apprenticeship in these institutions. Thus the talented individual who has followed the private path and who, by solitary work, has possibly gained more knowledge and probably achieved more originality than he would have done under a classroom routine, meets a barrier to that natural career in which he would have expressed himself and formed others in his own image.[3]

These ideas, colored no doubt by the "class assumptions" of the period, are further supported by Constant on the grounds that private education is in keeping with a widespread growth of independence of mind, and a calling in question of the authority of the state, which he discerned among his contemporaries.

It is consistent with what has been said so far that Constant should be anxious to prevent teachers from becoming mere tools of government policy. This is why he considers that while the state should provide material educational facilities, it should not appoint teachers. The same considerations make him recommend that teachers should be modestly paid. On the other hand, he argues that they should have generous pensions and enjoy security of tenure. A teacher will be dismissed only in the most exceptional circumstances. Should such circumstances arise, the case will be judged by wholly independent persons entirely free of any government connection.

Constant concludes by insisting that true educational progress is inseparable from individual freedom and that he looks for such progress in the private rather than the public sphere. The government must guard and preserve educational opportunity, but it must also remain neutral and allow each citizen freedom to follow his private truth and develop his talents in a genuine spirit of independence.

III *The Slave Trade*

The slave traffic of the seventeenth, eighteenth, and early nineteenth centuries was clearly one of the most outrageous and inhuman attacks on freedom. Constant regarded it as such and spoke repeatedly, and in forthright terms, on the subject, especially between 1821 and 1829. He described the slave trade, in a speech of June, 1821, as "the most atrocious crime of which an evil-doer can be guilty." The same speech ended with the passage:

Gentlemen, in the name of humanity, and on a subject which demands that all party differences be disregarded, join with me in demanding the law which the ministry promised us. Let us require, under threat of refusing to vote the sums asked of us, that the bill be presented in this present session. The session will be extended by a few days, but thousands of human beings will escape the fate with which a longer delay threatens them—and we shall not have called down on our own heads the responsibility for those atrocities which are being committed as I speak to you from this rostrum. Let us demand that this law above all suppresses an abuse which the minister admitted last year and seemed to regard as natural. When the English capture and confiscate slave ships, they free the slaves. When we asked the minister what happened to the Negroes confiscated in Senegal he replied that they became government property and were put to work in the colony. Gentlemen, a truth emerges from this quiet statement; it is that despite promises, treaties and royal decrees, the slave trade goes on and the government profits from it.[4]

As against this governmental inactivity of which he complained, Constant offered his fellow deputies documentary evidence of various atrocities. These included the throwing of thirty-nine Negroes overboard from a slave ship. The Negroes in question had become blind as a result of the appalling conditions in which they were kept. They thus became a mere liability and of no interest or value to prospective purchasers. On another occasion, when a ship was being searched for slaves by the authorities, the captain hid his human cargo, some of whom were children, in small wooden cases. A number of these cases were similarly thrown overboard, with their human contents, when the search became uncomfortably thorough.

It is characteristic of Constant that he does not simply throw up his hands in horror at this evidence, or confine himself to lecturing the government on morality. He is appalled, of course, but he also seeks a practical, effective solution. First of all, particularly in a speech of May, 1822, he points out that mere confiscation of the slave cargo will remain an ineffectual sanction while one successful and undetected voyage can produce a profit for the slavers of something between two hundred and three hundred percent. Furthermore, if a slave captain is caught, he is not prosecuted and fined, much less imprisoned. He loses his command, but goes completely free and can find alternative employment or retire on his considerable earnings. Constant contrasts this situation with the punishment meted out to those who commit petty thefts or express opinions hostile to the government of the day. He also points out that an English sea captain indulging in the slave trade is transported, on conviction, to the penal colony of Botany Bay. Finally, in his attempt to get more severe and more effective legislation against the traffic in slaves, he argues that to prohibit it in theory, yet not prevent it in practice, makes it even more cruel. This is mainly because the law can be circumvented, but the stratagems adopted to get round it are particularly callous where trade in human beings is concerned. Quite apart from this, Constant also emphasizes the high mortality rate on the slave ships because of the unbelievably cramped and unhygienic conditions. He points out that this mortality rate was accepted as a fact of life and regularly and automatically set against any calculation of profits.

At a more indirect level, but still with the need for practical arguments in mind, Constant also points out to his fellow deputies that the traffic in slaves is populating the colonies with enemies who will one day take a terrible revenge on their European exploiters. The example of San Domingo (Haiti) is in the forefront of his mind and particularly, one supposes, the ferocious killing on both sides that accompanied the Negro revolt of 1791. Elsewhere he refers to this incident and says: "Yes, the Negroes who broke their chains were ferocious; they punished fearful cruelty with fearful cruelty."

Constant's chapter on the slave trade in his *Commentaire* on Filangieri repeats a number of the points made above. He writes, for example: "The traffic in black slaves has become much more cruel since being hindered by ineffectual prohibitions." [5] In the same chapter he adds the point that the slave trade corrupts those who carry it on as well as those who are its victims.

For Constant, a further aspect of the moral problem posed by slavery arose from the fact that part of the European public continued to regard Negroes as animals rather than members of the human race. He adds:

This section of the public, which would blush at murder or robbery on the highway, does not scruple to take part in a commercial traffic which attracts it by the profit which results. It numbs its own sensibility with sophistries which seek to disguise the fact that there is at least equivalence between it and the murderer or the incendiary. When this truth is properly realized; when the law makes no distinction between crimes that are at least equal; when, independently of the law, outraged public opinion pursues in the streets and public squares any merchant who has taken part in the slave trade, then virtually the whole commercial population will refuse to be a party to it . . .

We must therefore work unceasingly to create this moral conviction. We must not simply confine ourselves, like Filangieri, to setting forth principles and proving that the slave trade is, theoretically, a violation of all rights. We must demonstrate with facts that it is, in practice, a bringing together of all crimes. We must reveal all the features of cruelty with which it sullies the maritime annals of all nations.[6]

Constant set an example to the public by the way in which he stuck to this task during the last ten years of his life. He did much to rouse public opinion and was fortified by the conviction that, since truth will always finally prevail, the abolition of the slave trade ("which, although it exists only in theory, is a striking demonstration of the all-powerful nature of truth") will eventually become operative in fact and not merely in theory.

IV   *Religious Freedom*

Pascal begins one of the longest and most profound fragments in his *Pensées* with a demand that those who attack religion should at least understand properly the object of their attack.[7] In a rather similar way, in his chapter on intolerance toward religion in the *Principes de politique* (Chapter XVII), Constant begins by declaring what religion is (in his view) before going on to argue that the antipathy and even persecution which it encounters are thoroughly unjustified.

Constant's approach is one which expresses strongly that *sensibilité* which existed side by side with his sharp intelligence. He claims, first of all, that religion offers a peculiarly effective form of human satisfaction. All enduring consolation has a religious foundation; a spiritual faith is, in his own words, *la compagne fidèle, l'ingénieuse et infatigable amie de l'infortuné.*[8] Obviously, this is a personal view which, while many would share it, many others would reject. Constant's second point has more widespread validity and is of considerable importance and interest. He argues, in effect, that all human experience contains elements which lie beyond the reach of rational analysis. This, he says, is particularly true of certain emotions which can be accounted for only in religious terms. He regards religious sentiment as an emotion which is inseparable from the most noble aspirations and the most profound feelings which we experience—love for another person, the ability to put the needs of others before our own, melancholy ("that motiveless sadness which also possesses an underlying pleasure which we cannot analyze"), and a thousand other sensations which cannot be adequately described or which elude rational explanation. In short, he believes in a close link between nobility, sensibility, and religious feeling. Consequently, religion, as he conceives it, is involved in raising us to the highest conception of ourselves.

Constant also links religious sentiment with beauty, because beauty, too, possesses a moral component. To contemplate the Apollo Belvedere, or a painting by Raphael, is to be taken outside or beyond ourselves by the spectacle of aesthetic perfection. Art can convince us that a perfection exists which is of more account than we are. By thus inspiring in us a momentary disinterestedness—even a fleeting glimpse of the eternal—it can arouse within us "that capacity for self-sacrifice which is the source of all virtue." [9]

At the same time, Constant does not claim that, in the case of a given individual, the absence of religious feeling automatically denotes an absence of morality. There are those whose minds are impervious to religion in any accepted form yet who live scrupulously moral lives based on reason. However, he does claim that those who practice virtue in the absence of religious conviction are a small intellectual and moral élite; for the vast majority of men this is simply not possible. Once again, of course, Constant is in part begging the question by leaving the nature of morality undefined or by restricting it to noble or profound emotions. His case is only internally consistent to the extent that he believed in a naturally corrupt human nature. He was honest enough—some might say cynical enough—to posit natural corruption on a number of occasions.

In contrast to egotism, moral failure, and short-sighted rational self-deception, religion is rooted in "that vague yet profound part of our moral feelings which, by its very nature, defies all attempts by language to encompass it." [10] Not to experience this religious sense is to be "deprived of a precious faculty and disinherited by Nature."

This exposition of the ineffable qualities of religious sensation ends with a passage which is worth quoting both because it conveys well the flavor of Constant's ideas and because it amounts to a striking expression of Romantic sensibility:

How will you define the impression created by a dark night, an age-old forest, the wind moaning through ruins or on gravestones, the ocean extending beyond our sight? How will you define the emotion caused in you by the songs of Ossian, the church of St. Peter, meditation on death, the harmony of sounds and shapes? How will you define reverie, that inner tremulousness of soul in which all the powers of feeling and thought meet and seemingly disperse in mysterious confusion? There is religion underlying all these things. Everything that is beautiful, everything that is profoundly personal, everything that is noble participates in religion. [11]

Having made this case for the all-pervasive and integral role of religious sentiment in much that we think finest in our human experience, Constant now goes on to ask why, in these circumstances, it has been the object of such bitter attacks. Furthermore, why have these attacks—often the prelude to gross interference with religious freedom—been so frequently mounted by particularly intelligent and well-educated people? His answer, as one might guess, is that true religion has been distorted and institutionalized by human agency (elsewhere he distinguishes clearly between *le sentiment religieux* and *les formes religieuses*). Institutional religion has frequently proved to be dogmatic and inflexible, menacing the simple-minded faithful and persecuting heretics and nonbelievers. On occasions it has become a worse evil than the evil it sought to combat. Constant thus sees many intolerant attitudes to religion as arising from a prior ecclesiastical intolerance. In a typically neat formulation, he says: "Intolerance, by putting force on the side of faith, put courage on the side of doubt." [12]

He expresses sadness and some astonishment at reading d'Holbach's attack on Christianity and religion generally in his *Système de la nature*. Yet although he thinks d'Holbach was wholly mistaken in his advocacy of atheism, he can understand this attitude, given the religious intolerance which d'Holbach experienced. Intellectual bullying and physical threats automatically provoke resistance on the part of courageous individuals. In many cases, of course, the disbelief occurs before the persecution, but if such disbelief were not immediately met by intolerance, many atheists and freethinkers would remain silent or apathetic. Some might even grow dissatisfied with their intellectual position.

The one way to ensure therefore that religion is not attacked is to see that it does not fall into the hands of authoritarian fanatics. Religious belief must be wholly a matter of freedom and never a question of constraint. Government interference with religion, whether in support or attack, is firmly condemned. We have already seen that Constant was strongly opposed to all governmental intervention in ideas. Hence he deplored the state assault on religion which followed 1789, but he was equally against later attempts by the government to resuscitate institutional religion in a skeptical age. Because authentic religious feelings are part and parcel of Nature, and because they are also an integral part of what is best in man, their expression must not be tampered with, either in defense or attack, by the voice of authority. Above all, true religion cannot be defended by men who do not share its ideals, but believe only in despotic power.

At this point, Constant goes on to criticize some of the traditional social arguments used in support of religion, arguments which he attacks because they can only finally weaken what they are designed to strengthen. It is alleged, for example, that "the common people need religion." Constant draws a severe constrast between the often obvious crimes of the poor and the sophisticated and concealed sins of an opulent artistocracy. Religion is therefore not "necessary,' is some exclusive way, for some single section of society only. If his account of it is right, it is something—he says—of which all men of all classes stand in need.

Similarly, he thinks that one can do only a disservice to religion by presenting it in more directly utilitarian terms. It is often advocated, for example, as a deterrent to crime generally, but for Constant it must never become "an auxiliary of the gallows and the rack." Religion, indeed, should be used to enhance virtue, not to repress crime. Also, at a more general level, all types of utilitarian argument render religion secondary to something else. In that sense, they finally degrade the very thing they seek to promote.

The health of religion is therefore linked in Constant's mind with complete freedom to express and practice one's religious beliefs. He holds that all sects should enjoy the same freedom and prefers a multiplicity of sects to one single denomination which quickly becomes formalistic, meaningless, and corrupt. "When religion degenerates in this way it loses all moral influence; it becomes lodged, as it were, in a pigeonhole of the mind where it is isolated from all the rest of existence. In Italy we see the mass precede murder, confession follow it, penitence absolve it and a man, thus freed from remorse, contemplate further murders." [13] In favor of a multiplicity of religious groupings, Constant adds the point that many new sects arise from a strong and positive moral reaction to the real or alleged laxity of the parent denomination. To this extent, the growth of new sects favors increased moral concern and may even induce a new awareness of ethical standards in the parent grouping ("the appearance of Protestantism reformed the morals of the Catholic clergy").

Constant's conclusion, then, is that no religion should be proscribed, even if it appears to constitute some sort of danger. In keeping with his ideas on press censorship, he considers that actions should be punished only when they infringe the law and not because they exceed the limits of accepted religious orthodoxy. To attack the clergy in particular, as happened after 1789, is to give birth, eventually, to a much wider surge of lay sympathy, even by non-Christians, on behalf of these victims of persecution.

In a brief final paragraph, Constant returns to the need to keep all religions free from state interference: "What applies to the highways applies to religion: I like the state to keep them in good repair, provided it grants everyone the right to prefer other roads." [14]

V *Individual Freedom*

It is clear that individual freedom is the focal point of Constant's intellectual theory and social practice. His views on the press, education, the slave trade, and the organization of religion are all based on this central consideration. All forms of freedom are interrelated, and their final justification is the degree of liberty which they confer on the *individual*. In an important sense, then, individual freedom has been the real subject of the preceding sections of this chapter. However, since Constant also wrote about it as a separate topic, it is worth glancing very quickly at what he had to say.

There is a short chapter on individual freedom in the *Principes de politique* (Chapter XVIII). It begins with the statement that while all French constitutions have guaranteed personal liberty, in practice these guarantees have been repeatedly violated. Now, because freedom and morality, according to Constant, are inseparable, to violate one is to violate the other. Morality requires security if it is to be exercised at either the private or public level. Any interference with freedom inevitably lessens that security. Therefore, to interfere with freedom is to undermine moral standards. He draws a parallel with the collapse of morality in times of plague (e.g., the Black Death) and goes on to make his by now familiar criticisms of the "plague" of arbitrary government: it creates injustice through a capricious use of arrest and imprisonment; it deprives judges of independent authority; it has recourse to deportation without proper trial; it acts against individuals (and groups) without providing either explanation or justification. Repeatedly during his life, Constant wrote and spoke against these arbitrary procedures and in defense of individuals victimized by them.

In conclusion, it should be said that Constant's liberalism, which crystallized round the notion of personal freedom, was at bottom emotional rather than intellectual. It was born of a particular feeling for, and imaginative identification with, the sufferings of others. He put the emotional basis of his own liberalism succinctly when he wrote: "Suffering sometimes arouses in us what is most noble in our nature: courage, and sometimes what is most tender: sympathy and pity. It teaches us to fight on our own behalf and to feel for others." [15] Constant possessed both the courage and the pity which he mentions here. He exercised both in an unwearied defense of freedom.

CHAPTER 5

Anatomy of Religion

WHERE a sudden and radical change takes place in an individual's spiritual life, the direction is most frequently from skepticism toward belief. From St. Paul onward, the world is full of examples of conversion of the Damascus road type. On the other hand, where the change is much more gradual and includes a strongly intellectual element, the more common direction taken is from an earlier belief towards an increasingly settled skepticism. In the case of Constant's attitude to religion, however, we find that his experience appears to deny the usual configuration of both these categories. He certainly did not undergo a sudden, memorable conversion or illumination. Rather, he moved slowly, but also firmly and distinctly, from strong initial skepticism to a positive religious position. He gradually found the resolutely secular and rationalistic attitudes of the Enlightenment inadequate in terms of his own thought and experience. Having decided, early in his intellectual career, to argue the case for the superiority of paganism over Christianity, he ended by publishing a large-scale work in which he showed that religion at large, and Christianity in particular, were vital and central elements in human life.

For close on a hundred years, the religious side of Constant's nature and the significance of his views and writings on religion were largely ignored. Sainte-Beuve at least recognized the presence of some interest in religion, even if he harshly characterized it as "religiosity without faith," but Faguet was more representative with his claim that Constant entirely lacked any religious sense. It is only relatively recently that new work, particularly by Deguise, Hogue, Thompson, and Gouhier [1] has redirected attention toward this aspect of his life and ideas which Constant himself regarded as central.

Henri Gouhier [2] has rightly pointed out that the French

Revolution had quite crucial moral and religious consequences, as well as social and political ones. Indeed, religion and politics were closely related (often antithetically) in Revolutionary theory and practice which aimed, among other things, at establishing a new post-Christian religion of freedom, equality, and fraternity. Although institutional religion was thoroughly discredited in the eyes of many, the necessity for some form of religion—possibly a "religion of humanity"—remained. The choice facing an intellectual élite was put very clearly by De Maistre in 1797: "A true philosopher must choose between these two assumptions—either that a new religion will take shape, or that Christianity will be rejuvenated in some extraordinary manner." [3]

One of the best-known attempts to formulate a new religion was the instituting of the worship of Reason. The ground was prepared in part by such writers as Dupuis and Volney, the former of whom regarded religion as nothing more than a primitive, prescientific form of knowledge. Later, Comte was to move in the same direction, proposing a Religion of Humanity (later described by T. H. Huxley as "Catholicism without God") as appropriate to the new scientific age. On the other hand, the creation of a renewed and revitalized Christianity also had its advocates. These included the mystic and illuminist Saint-Martin and, of course, Chateaubriand. The latter's *Génie du christianisme* presented Christianity as being of unique and continuing relevance in human affairs. And although so many of Constant's views were different from those of Chateaubriand, he too belongs to the category of Christian renovators. Like Chateaubriand, he took an evolutionary approach to religion and saw a purified and "reasonable" Christianity as the final flowering of centuries of human endeavour and aspiration.

I Rationalist Beginnings

Constant was brought up in the intellectual traditions of the French *philosophes*. He tells us in *Le Cahier rouge* that he read voraciously as a boy, absorbing a materialist and rationalist philosophy in a variety of eighteenth-century works ranging from the writings of La Mettrie to the novels of Crébillon. We also know that the Constant family had earlier established personal links with Voltaire and his influence was exceeded only by that of Montesquieu in terms of scope and duration. Lesser *philos-*

ophes who nevertheless contributed markedly to Constant's early intellectual formation included Helvétius and d'Holbach. Constant refers to the former in *Le Cahier rouge* and indicates something of the influence which *De l'esprit* exercised over him at the age of eighteen: "Having been brought up on the principles of eighteenth-century philosophy, and more particularly on the works of Helvétius, my sole thought was to make my contribution to the destruction of what I called prejudices." [4] This was written in 1811, referring to the period 1784–85, and the change in Constant's attitude, which we shall discuss shortly, is implied by the tone of his further comment: "I had seized on an assertion by the author of *De l'esprit* to the effect that pagan religion was greatly to be preferred to Christianity. I wished to support this assertion, which I had neither studied thoroughly nor examined critically, with some facts chosen at random and with many epigrams and declamatory statements which I thought were novel."

This passage suggests Constant's later reservations toward one of his early philosophical mentors. Indeed, he became positively critical of most Enlightenment thinkers though his admiration for Montesquieu, whose influence was political rather than metaphysical, remained unaffected. In some ways he was permanently marked by eighteenth-century rationalism, but the story of his life up to 1807 is the story of a gradual emancipation from those antireligious assumptions which characterized the age. Evidence is not lacking concerning his religious ideas and attitudes during adolescence and early manhood. At the same time, the available evidence is scattered and fragmentary, scarcely providing a very coherent picture. Nevertheless, one can trace a general, if somewhat erratic, movement from initial agnosticism and even antagonism to religion to something approaching a later conversion. In the course of this development he went through some complex intermediate stages including a period of nihilism, a desire for faith which still eluded fulfillment, and a handling of skepticism in such a way that it was finally and paradoxically transformed into an instrument of belief.

Constant's early antagonism to Christianity is indicated in the passage from the *Cahier rouge* quoted above. Around the same period, during a stay with the Suard family in Paris, he met a number of *philosophes* personally and was further confirmed in his ideas. Nevertheless, his positive secularism and atheism were not accompanied by the fundamental optimism which characterizes much eighteenth-century thought. Partly, he seems to have lacked the necessary temperamental equipment; partly, his private experiences, together with the influence of Mme de Charrière, contributed to an increasing sense of gloom. In one of his letters of 1790 to Mme de Charrière, part of which was quoted in Chapter 1, he refers to a *vexation perpétuelle de près de trois ans.* Another letter of the same year included a revealing and well-known passage:

I feel more than ever the nullity of everything—the extent to which everything contains promise but nothing offers fulfillment, the extent to which our powers are greater than what we accomplish, and how much the disparity between these two things is bound to make us miserable . . .

Constant then puts forward, with approval, an idea suggested by an Italian friend, the chevalier de Revel:

He [Revel] claims that God, the author of our lives and our surroundings, died before He finished His work; . . . that everything is now made for a purpose which no longer exists and that we ourselves, in particular, feel destined for something which we are incapable of conceiving. We resemble watches without faces, containing works endowed with intelligence which would go on moving until they were worn out, without knowing why and saying continually to each other: "Since I move, I must have a purpose." This idea strikes me as the most witty and profound madness I have ever heard, and greatly preferable to the Christian, Muslim and philosophic madnesses of the 1st, 6th and 18th centuries.[5]

Almost exactly a year later, in 1791, Constant was again expressing his agnosticism, verging on atheism, in forthright terms to Mme de Charrière. In the course of arguing that things are arranged satisfactorily for the preservation of the human species, but very badly for the happiness of individuals, he includes the phrase: ". . . God, if He exists, something which I grow to doubt more and more as time goes on . . ."[6]

Constant's gloom and near nihilism of this period were intensified by the double nature of his skepticism. We have seen him implying rejection both of first-century Christian folly and eighteenth-century philosophic madness. Other letters written about the same time show that, while he could not accept the "preposterous and mysterious" promises of a religion which struck him as absurd, he had also lost confidence in Enlightenment ideals and could not believe in the hopes entertained by a rationalist and materialist philosophy "composed merely of words." To believe neither in God nor man was a position which he could not sustain indefinitely. His wish for a form of positive belief became increasingly strong. It is not surprising, then, that we should find him writing in 1792: "I can see no proof, no probability, that there is a God, although I swear that I would really want there to be one. Such a thing would change my whole existence. . . . I see that morality is vague, that man is wicked, weak, stupid and base, and I believe that such is his destiny." [7] During the years which immediately followed, these religious and philosophical problems of Constant's were temporarily submerged by his absorbing relationship with Mme de Staël and his active political theorizing. They were never far below the surface, however, and came to a head again in 1807.

II *Mystical Renunciation*

At this point, Constant had reached an intellectual impasse. The fact that he referred several times to his incapacity for belief reveals at the very least the outlines of an underlying religious sensibility. On the other hand, the skepticism which made orthodox religious teaching alien to him also prevented him from finding consolation in Enlightenment rationalism. In a sense, he actually used the *philosophes'* main instrument of destruction against themselves. The incredulity which led them to scorn Christianity made his own resistance to Christianity less strong once he had turned this incredulity, in a critical spirit, against their narrowly rationalist attacks on religion. In these circumstances, the compromise of deism was not a serious possibility. His position was one from which it was impossible to break out by purely intellectual means.

Eventually, Constant escaped from a daunting intellectual dilemma by turning to mysticism. One should not be surprised, given his complex and contradictory nature, that religious mysticism appealed to that side of him which displayed a notable element of sensibility, even sentimentality, and which had been encouraged by Mme de Staël's enthusiasm for the more emotional aspects of the German national character. More particularly, the mystical ideas which he met in the Quietist movement, with its emphasis on extinction of the will and complete abandonment to the Divine Presence, were in keeping with the intense feelings of intellectual helplessness and *taedium vitae* which he frequently experienced.

It is clear that Constant's enthusiasm for Quietism was not the outcome of a slowly evolving development. On the contrary, his new religious sensibility was a rather sudden change of direction—what he himself called a "graft." In a letter of 1807 to his aunt, the comtesse de Nassau, he wrote: "Religion possesses the admirable quality—I say this in all seriousness—it possesses the admirable quality of not being adversely affected by what precedes it. One can graft it onto ambition, onto love, onto all passions, and the graft takes at any age." [8] He was aware that the religious attitude of willing renunciation and devotion which he now adopted from the Quietists was being grafted onto his own secular feeling of world weariness and despair. As a result, a (temporary) sense of deliverance and consolation flowed through his whole being like the sap in a newly grafted plant.

In the summer of 1807, during a stay in Lausanne, Constant made contact (not, in fact, for the first time) with the Quietist sect there known as "Les Ames intérieures." A number of his relatives were members, including the chevalier Charles de Langallerie who played a leading role in the group. While the intellectual and spiritual difficulties already mentioned make it understandable that Constant should have been interested in this small band of mystics, his immediate impulse probably had more to do with the crisis in his emotional life. He was caught between his responsibilities and feelings toward Mme de Staël and Charlotte von Hardenberg much in the way described—between Mme de Malbée and Cécile—in his transparently autobiographical novel, *Cécile*. In the sixth of the seven *époques* into which this novel is divided, there is a lengthy passage on his contacts with the "Ames intérieures." Having briefly explained that their ideas were derived from the late seventeenth-century teachings of Fénelon and Mme Guyon, he

[92]

summarizes the advice he received from the sect to pray and to renounce his own will.

The practice of prayer is not something easily associated with Constant at this stage, and he tells us that a leading personality from the group said to him: "You will make the objection: 'How can one pray when one does not believe?' I can only reply: 'Try it and you will see, ask and you will receive.'" [9] Constant took this advice and also read several works by Mme Guyon. He obtained a strangely consoling peace as a result, and tells us: "I made it a rule to live from day to day, without concerning myself either about what had happened, since it was past help, or about what was going to happen, since it had to be left unreservedly to the ordering of Him who arranges everything." Each of his prayers ended with the words: "I completely abjure all my faculties, all knowledge, all reason, all judgment." Finally, he writes significantly: "The majority of the dogmas which I had rejected —the existence of God, the immortality of the soul—appeared to me not to be demonstrated by logic but proved by a kind of inner experience. I did not measure these dogmas with the eternally inaccurate instrument of reason, but experienced them as true and irrefutable." Constant's *Journal* for the same period is less definite than this, but if it contains frequent references to *la destinée* and *le ciel*, it also invokes *la Providence* and *Dieu bon et compatissant*. What he chiefly obtained from the Quietists of Lausanne was a religious emotion which, by its mystical character, bypassed his intellectual problems but really left them untouched and unsolved.

III *The Claims of Feeling and Reason*

Constant's sincerity during the Lausanne episode is not in doubt. There is a considerable change in his attitude to religion from this point onward. While he was always able to understand and sympathize with sincere and intelligent agnosticism, he never again returned to what he described as "that narrow and cynical philosophy which in Voltaire saw us as being born between urine and fecal matter, in Helvétius distinguished us from horses only by our hands, in Diderot wished to strangle the last priest with the bowels of the last king, and in Cabanis defined thought as a secretion of the brain." [10] This is from a letter of 1811 to Prosper de Barante. On 21 October 1808, to the same correspondent, he had expressed his conviction that a great religious surge was discernible among his contemporaries and that religion had forsaken discredited outward forms to dwell the more securely within men's hearts. There may be some truth in the suggestion that Constant wrote to Barante the kind of things the latter wanted to hear; nevertheless, there is no reason to doubt his statement made two days later: "My religion consists of two things: to will what God wills, that is to say to give Him the homage of our hearts; and to deny nothing, that is to say to give Him the homage of our minds." [11] The Quietist emphasis of these words is further confirmed by the sentence which follows: "Given these two points, the way is established from earth to heaven and each on his own account finds this path surrounded by protection, inner consolation and a particular providence which none can prove but which is felt at each step."

Constant referred to this approach as "experimental" or "experiential" religion. In his *Benjamin Constant méconnu*, Pierre Deguise [12] has included some interesting and previously unpublished fragments by Constant on this subject. In one of these, he insists that his religious views amount neither to a system nor a coherent doctrine, but simply reflect facts met with in the act of living. His religion, he says, is wholly a matter of personal experience. Consequently he adds: "I do not take offense when I see it treated as daydreaming by those who have never had such an experience."

However, although Constant was sincere, and although he turned to another form of religious mysticism in 1815, he was not by temperament a natural mystic. By 1811, during a stay in Göttingen with Charlotte, he was working again on his historical study of religion. He certainly now conceived of his task in a very different spirit from that in which he had begun the work twenty-five years earlier, but the nature of the enterprise, and the German intellectual circles in which he moved, encouraged a philosophical and historical approach which would have been quite alien to the "Ames intérieures." By this time he had read widely among many different German philosophers and theologians including Kant, Herder, Voss, Schelling, Fichte, Heyne, Creuzer, Goerres, and Berger. During the next couple of years he also read the Church Fathers and the Bible. Of the latter he noted in his *Journal* for February 1813 that it had overturned all his ideas. Indeed, this is a period during which his writings on religion changed a great deal both in general outline and specific detail.

It is worth quoting at this point Constant's own account of his religious development up to 1811 and his oscillation between feeling and reason, enthusiasm and demonstration. The passage is a long one from the letter written to Prosper de Barante on 2 December 1811. It precedes the description of eighteenth-century philosophy as "narrow and cynical" quoted at the beginning of this section. Interestingly enough, Constant starts with the claim that the more facts he accumulated, with the original intention of attacking religion, the more convinced he became, once he had faced the evidence of these facts fairly and squarely, that religion should be preserved and fostered. This new religious conviction, predicated on positive historical fact rather than negative mystical retreat, also enabled him to give greater shape and coherence—as well as a new argument and emphasis—to the work on religion which he was writing:

My work will certainly accord with your views. I have been led to this position by innumerable facts which I have interpreted with all the more impartiality because I collected them with contrary ideas in mind. For a long time, my own habits, and the direction taken by my thoughts, caused me to do some sort of violence to these facts in order to match them to the purpose of my enterprise. However, since I was sincere, this violence had no effect. The proofs recoiled on me, the human heart was revealed for what it is when religious feeling is banished from it, and religious sentiment alone could not satisfy me for long since it is vague and powerless when left to itself. I saw skeptical man rushing headlong after magic. I saw man fatigued by skepticism and only able to replace it by ecstasy, unbridled enthusiasm, and exaggerated ideas that were all the more incurable because they began with reasoning and advanced methodically towards madness. I saw reason in all its splendor and all its weakness, four centuries of thought amounting first and foremost to chaos, a fantastic and arbitrary arrangement of affairs with man succeeding in destroying everything but incapable of restoring anything. Finally yielding to such irresistible evidence, I saw God as providing man not only with religion but with reason itself.

Since freely admitting these truths to myself, a strangely wonderful simplicity has been diffused through my work. Suddenly my path, obscure for so many years, revealed itself as clear and smooth. I saw all my ideas fall into a pattern which all my efforts up to that point had failed to discover. I saw the solutions to difficult problems.

German philosophy helps me a great deal although it is not developing in quite the same direction as my own. It follows a line from which I have deviated, but which is nevertheless a parallel line. . . . It is a somewhat vague philosophy, but it respects the religious element everywhere, finding in religion everything that is good and becoming agitated only in its attempts to generalize its ideas and locate the divine in everything in order to achieve a more attractive result by its apparent universality.[13]

Nevertheless, within a few years, renewed emotional pressures caused Constant to deviate from his own path again and to seek escape and consolation in another form of mysticism.

IV Prayers and Miracles

We saw that Constant's mystical "crisis" of 1807 was motivated, in part at least, by the difficulties of his emotional life and particularly by his complicated relationships with Mme de Staël and Charlotte von Hardenberg. The sublimation of passion in religion is not an unusual phenomenon, and attention has often been drawn to the links which appear to exist between sexual attitudes and mystical beliefs and practices. The 1807 situation is therefore not surprising, nor is the fact that Constant's painful relationship with Mme Récamier was followed by a renewed turning to mysticism in 1815. Indeed, by the late summer of 1815, he was in a state of deep depression, further intensified by political disappointments, and had considered the possibility of suicide on at least two occasions. His *Journal* for September of that year clearly reflects his state of mind and also records his first contacts with the celebrated mystic and prophetess Mme de Krüdener. Her name occurs in virtually every second entry throughout the month and for part of October in terms of conversations held, letters exchanged, prayers said together, and attempts to exercise a beneficent influence on Juliette Récamier.

Baroness von Krüdener, whose novel *Valérie* had been severely criticized by Constant in 1804, became converted in her forties to a suspect form of mysticism. She traveled throughout Europe preaching her ideas and claiming miracles, and achieved considerable political influence as a result of her association with

Tsar Alexander I. She was a moving spirit in the conception of the Holy Alliance of 1815. This was a group of sovereigns (in Russia, Austria, and Prussia) who undertook to rule by Christian principles. Significantly, the Holy Alliance was termed by Lord Castlereagh "a piece of sublime mysticism and nonsense."

As regards his personal contacts with Mme de Krüdener, Constant remained chiefly conscious of the sublimity, though he was not unaware of the nonsense. His very first note, of 4 September, contains a comment on his *conversation religieuse* with Mme de Krüdener to the effect that he was moved by the content but disliked the form in which it was put, and particularly the emphasis on miracles.[14] Later, on 11 October, we find him complaining that members of Mme de Krüdener's circle describe paradise as though it were their own bedroom; why, he asks, should they forsake authentic feeling for puerile description?[15] Nevertheless, although one may dislike the apparent self-consciousness of Constant's references to having "religious" conversations or writing "religious" letters, it is clear that he derived considerable comfort from the practice of prayer and from discussions with Mme de Krüdener herself. We read such phrases as *Je me suis soumis. J'ai prié et j'ai éprouvé une douleur douce,* or *Mon intérieur est plus calme et plus doux. . . .*[16]

During his consultations with Mme de Krüdener, Constant did not forget his original motive. While offering up prayers in which he renounced will, ambition and pride, he continued to hope that his mystical friend would be instrumental in creating a unity of souls between Mme Récamier and himself. Even before revealing fully the details of his feelings for Juliette, he had emphasized the dire nature of his problem in the course of a letter—a typical blend of emotion and irony—to Mme de Krüdener: "You told me that I had a right to miracles performed by you. God forbid that I should demand some and tempt the Divine Goodness! But if you can perform some miracles, carry one out in order to save me. Time is pressing."[17] In the event, he made various attempts to secure Juliette's conversion to Mme de Krüdener's illuminist ideas, even bringing her to prayer sessions in the latter's home, but he continued to find her "little suited to religious ideas." However, whether as a result of prayers, a miracle or human mutability, Constant had largely recovered by the end of October from his passion for Juliette. He recovered likewise from this second short bout of mysticism, though he continued to think well of Mme de Krüdener.

From this point onward there were no further dramatic developments, in biographical terms, in Constant's religious odyssey. He continued to emphasize the importance of the religious instinct in man, defended the religious sense against rationalist attack, and pursued his own research and writing in connection with his historical study of religion.

V The Historical Study of Religion

In a letter of 11 October 1811 written to Claude Hochet,[18] Constant quoted Bacon's famous statement in his essay "Of Atheism": "It is true, that a little philosophy inclineth Man's mind to atheism, but depth in philosophy bringeth men's minds about to religion." He went on to explain, as we have already seen him do at the same period to Prosper de Barante, that the more facts he accumulated for his work on religion, the more they destroyed the skepticism and even antagonism with which he had begun. As a result, what started as an attempt to demonstrate the superiority of paganism over Christianity ended as a study of the gradual growth and increasing perfection of religious ideas through the stages of fetishism, polytheism, and monotheism. Constant believed that this process of growth and refinement was bringing religion increasingly nearer to a final truth which it would eventually attain once it reflected directly the emotional power and the (difficult) moral simplicity of the gospels. After a lifetime of reflection and patient research, he set out these ideas in detail in *De la religion, considérée dans sa source, ses formes et ses développements*, published in five volumes between 1824 and 1831, and *Du polythéisme romain, considéré dans ses rapports avec la philosophie grecque et la religion chrétienne* (*On Roman Polytheism*), posthumously published in two volumes in 1833.

It is usual to dismiss these two works as thoroughly outdated and of interest only in so far as they throw light on Constant's more immediately personal views. While it is true that they do possess this particular interest for the modern reader, it is also worth pointing out that they are the result of impressively deep and wide-ranging erudition on Constant's part. Obviously, he could not be expected to anticipate the findings of modern scholarship in the fields of anthropology, classical studies, comparative religion, and philology. What he says about the religion of the Chaldeans or the Egyptians is now out of date, and his knowledge of Indian religion was severely limited, but the general evolution of religious ideas which he traces, from early times to the present, remains basically acceptable and of considerable interest. He rightly saw religion as something eternally changing in its external forms, but static, profound, and universal in its essential content. He did not hesitate to place Christianity in a wide historical and comparative context. He resisted contemporary attempts to reduce religion to something purely secular by "arguing it away" in terms of fear, superstition, ignorance, etc. He argued strongly for a "free" and "personal" religion untrammeled by the undesirable aspects of priestly domination. Not least, he pitted the Christian ethic against the doctrine of "enlightened self-interest" propounded by Helvétius, and against ethical utilitarianism generally.

Constant did not find it easy to give satisfactory shape to these ideas. He gradually accumulated an enormous amount of material which, even when systematically arranged, did not fall readily into a clear pattern. As a result, the story of the writing of these books is in part a story of repeated changes and new overall plans. While it would not be appropriate to go into these changes here,[19] it is understandable that the necessarily intermittent nature of his work over forty years, together with fundamental alterations in his own religious ideas and a conscientious concern to give the whole matter the most effective treatment possible, inevitably involved many hesitations and revisions.

Initially, Constant embarked on a general study of polytheism. For many years he referred in his *Journal* to his notes and papers on religion as "Polythéisme." He did so, indeed, long after he had begun a much wider analysis of religious phenomena, so that the term "Polythéisme" became a misleading shorthand title for something very different. Where critics tend to disagree, however, is on the nature of the connection between the two volumes on Roman polytheism and the five volumes of the main study of religion. It would be difficult to deny that *Du polythéisme romain* stands as a complete work on its own even if it contains complete passages already used in *De la religion* (this "self-plagiarism" is a characteristic of Constant's writings and particularly noticeable in several of his political works). At the same time, *Du polythéisme romain* is connected with *De la religion* in a more general sense, since it examines the collapse of paganism—something immediately relevant to *De la religion* but not expanded upon there.

Given this fact, and also bearing in mind the limited space available, it seems sensible to treat these two works together, looking at some of their main ideas on religion within the wider framework of fetishism, polytheism, and monotheism.

VI *Fetishism*

Fetishism, polytheism, and monotheism are different manifestations of a basic religious sense, and it is with this latter phenomenon that Constant begins. We saw in the previous chapter that he regarded it as a universal human feeling and considered it to be the source of some of man's highest moral aspirations and achievements. In the first volume of *De la religion*, he emphasizes its persistence throughout all ages and among all peoples. As evidence of its roots in the earliest forms of human consciousness, he instances the primitive savage who must struggle hard to obtain the minimum of food for mere subsistence, yet who gives to his fetish a portion of this hard-won food. In fact, something of the strength of this religious sense is seen in the way in which it often runs counter to one's immediate material interests.

By fetishism Constant means the worship by primitive peoples of inanimate objects or animals, which they believe to be inhabited by spirits. Fetishism, we might say, is a crude form of spirituality which precedes the nonreligious sentiments of fear, superstition, self-interest, etc. It shows us that the religious sense has an original tendency to "spiritualize" the material world. Later in the first volume, Constant argues that man experiences a fundamental need to enter into communication with the natural world surrounding him and with the mysterious powers which appear to animate it. Also, although fetishism is a crude phenomenon born in part of intellectual inadequacy, it is important in so far as it requires the primitive individual to perform certain self-denying actions and thus introduces a basic sense of ethical conduct into his life. The fetishist does not necessarily worship what he fears; he often bows down to objects which neither intimidate him nor offer him some practical advantage. For Constant, the initial instinct of primitive man is a wholly justified one. But since his reasoning powers are not highly developed, he has a very unsophisticated conception of spirituality and, in fetishism, his lack of knowledge misleads him concerning the causes of physical phenomena.

As regards the worship of animals, Constant emphasizes the fact that animals possess certain senses or faculties to a much greater degree of perfection than man. From different points of view they are both superior and inferior to him. Unable to explain their existence and purpose, and impressed by their strength or skill, the primitive mind sees some of them as the habitation of invisible spirits. Again, however, utility is not necessarily the motivating force of this interpretation. Constant suggests, for example, that the snake may well have earned religious respect, and subsequently become a major element in the mythologies of various peoples, not because it inspired fear, but because of the subtle interplay of its colors, the elusive sheen of its scales, the complex rapidity of its movements.

For Constant, primitive religion invests the physical world with a sense of the mysterious and secret, the animate and potent. It expresses, at an elementary level, that sense of the coexistence of material and spiritual life, of visible and invisible worlds, which is essential to the growth of more sophisticated religious and philosophical thought.[20] As against this potential development, however, another tendency works in the opposite direction. Primitive man, having identified a powerful spirit to his own satisfaction, tries to influence this spirit to his personal advantage. At this point, according to Constant, he is motivated by intelligent self-interest rather than by a properly religious spirit—and this is true of the rites (sacrifices, etc.) in which he subsequently indulges. Hence we find in outward religious forms and practices, from a very early stage, a rational, calculating element which Constant criticizes and deplores. The instinct to worship is a natural one, but it often finds expression in suspect or degenerate forms lacking any authentic religious quality.

VII *Polytheism*

In turning from fetishism to polytheism, we follow a gradual progress from primitive to higher religious forms. The higher religions (polytheism and monotheism) have grown out of more primitive antecedents and exhibit, in however altered a way, traces of this lineage.

It is usual to account for the movement away from fetishism and toward polytheism in social terms. The change from tribal to national patterns and the importance of agriculture are reflected in the advance from a conception of vague powers and capricious demons to the postulation of divine beings possessing specific qualities and distinct spheres of activity. This is a view which Constant appears to have anticipated,[21] though he sees the North American Indian worship of the Great Spirit, existing side by side with fetishism, as an intermediate stage on the way to a polytheistic hierarchy. He discerns a slowly evolving intellectual and artistic process at work, as well as social change, and says that the impulse behind the elaborately embellished fetishes and idols of primitive peoples eventually found more perfect expression in the Olympian Jupiter of Phidias.

It is in the third and fourth volumes of *De la religion* that Constant comments on the passage from fetishism to polytheism. He distinguishes between "independent" polytheism, which he admires, and "sacerdotal" polytheism, which he criticizes severely. He tells us that independent polytheism, as manifested in Greek culture, appeared in its infancy in Homeric poetry, made some advance in Hesiod, was further purified by Aeschylus, and attained perfection in Sophocles. Polytheism is the theatre of a continuing struggle between the mind, which seeks to separate and categorize, and the soul, which attempts to reconcile and unify. Hence the Greeks, out of a mistaken anthropomorphism, often attributed immoral qualities and actions to individual deities, but made "an imposing and respectable body" of the gods taken as a whole. Hence, also, the occasional sense of monotheism within polytheism—a sense which finally replaced the latter by the former when the intellect eventually "took some great steps forward." In the meantime, although polytheism remained a system full of contradictions, it contributed to the moral advance of man: "In trying to imagine the gods clothed in all the beauty, majesty and virtue that he could conceive, [man] had practice in meditating on these things and his moral sense benefited from his meditations." [22]

As regards sacerdotal polytheism—polytheism presided over

by a powerful priesthood—Constant criticizes it, again in Volumes Three and Four. He argues that independent polytheism virtually put an end to fetishism whereas, in sacerdotal polytheism, fetishism continued to exist in the form of idolatry. Furthermore, not only did the priesthood discourage an aesthetic sense which flourished under independent polytheism, the priests also discouraged attempts (as certain oriental religions show) to conceive of the gods in anything resembling human terms. They did so in order to inspire an awe which could be exploited in the interests of their own powerful and authoritarian status. They attributed various mysterious qualities to the gods and, inevitably, claimed a privileged understanding of these qualities. As a result, the gods of sacerdotal polytheism possessed grotesque and intimidating features which perverted their moral influence on credulous worshipers. They were vestiges of the more debased forms of fetishism and were often characterized by cruelty and indecency.

Apart from the moral deterioration introduced directly into polytheism by a self-perpetuating priesthood, Constant compares the sacerdotal unfavorably with the independent form from a more general intellectual standpoint. He holds that the tendency to arrest religion within the confines of superstition and fear caused it to become increasingly divorced from other ideas and from intellectual progress at large. Men's minds were diverted from the path of progress into obscure fantasy worlds, or encouraged to fall back on primitive ideas beyond which they had earlier advanced. Independent polytheism, on the contrary, was free to change in a way that reflected general intellectual growth. It remained in conformity with the intellectual changes of the day and was thus susceptible of further development. As he puts it: "No alien power obstructed progress." Thus if early Greek polytheism was crude in many ways, it nevertheless contained an important element of perfectibility which was effectively stifled in the sacerdotal form.

The fact that human beings were prepared, under sacerdotal polytheism, to worship imperfect, corrupt, or maleficent gods is interpreted by Constant, with more enthusiasm than justification, as further proof of the natural and ineradicable nature of religious feeling in mankind. He states: "The absurdity of certain religious forms, far from constituting an argument against religion, is a demonstration of the fact that we find it indispensable." [23]

The two forms of polytheism distinguished by Constant come together in the religion of Rome at the height of its glory. He traces the independent form to Greek influence and the sacerdotal to the earlier indigenous religion of Italy. Having examined both forms in some detail, he comes to the conclusion (in *Du polythéisme romain*, Book I, Chapter 10) that Roman polytheism represents the most highly developed form of belief in a plurality of gods. This is the polytheism which had the greatest influence for good on the minds, manners, and passions of its adherents. It both strengthened moral life and guaranteed the political constitution of the country. Characteristically, Constant reverts to the idea of freedom when he adds: "Thus Roman polytheism, by means of its invisible and mysterious power, protected institutions which were no doubt imperfect but which will certainly gain our respect when we reflect that a great people owed them six centuries of freedom." [24] By this stage polytheism had developed from a primitive belief in isolated and ill-defined deities to the worship of gods become "infinite in their qualities, and inconceivable in their essences."

VIII *Monotheism*

It is also in *Du polythéisme romain* that Constant examines the reasons for the decline and disappearance, in Europe at least, of polytheistic beliefs. The main factors, each of which he discusses at some length, are: confusion arising from a plurality of gods; increasing conflict between intellectual advance and polytheistic dogma; the transmutation of polytheism into allegory; the increasing ability of men to offer physical explanations of allegedly mysterious phenomena; the exploitation of polytheism by the priesthood for nonreligious ends; the secularization of religion in its conflicts with political powers; the growth of philosophy; the incoherence inherent in religious mysteries; the growth of magical practices. In much of this, of course, Constant lays considerable blame on the activities of the priesthood.

For Constant, the collapse of polytheism was inevitable in any case, given the fact that it was defended "violently but ineptly by authority, scandalously and without conviction by priests, weakly and indecisively by those philosophers devoted to its cause." [25] Furthermore, he regards the disappearance of polytheism as definitive since it depended on an ignorance concerning the nature of the physical world which was unavoidable in classical times but has long since given way to greater scientific understanding.

Despite this fact, however, Constant does not regard the intellectual inadequacies of polytheism as constituting a serious argument against the religious instinct as such. They simply mean that this particular *expression* of religious feeling was rightly shown to be inadequate and was obliged to give way to more refined and intellectually satisfactory forms.

The most refined form of all is monotheism, referred to as *théisme* by Constant. In *De la religion* he traces one of its origins to the Great Spirit or Manitou of the North American Indians. He also has a good deal to say, especially in the third volume, about the (limited) place of monotheism in Egyptian and oriental Indian religion. As regards the more specific question of progress from polytheism to monotheism, this is dealt with in the second volume of *Du polythéisme romain.*

For Constant, the coming of monotheism represents one of the most important revolutions in the history of human thought. He accepts the fact that it has often been associated with great intolerance (e.g., in its Muslim and Christian forms), but the decline of polytheism must still be seen as a great intellectual advance. Indeed, the very intellectual factors which sealed the fate of polytheism encouraged and guided the formulation of monotheistic doctrines. In addition, two other developments confirmed this general movement. One was a widespread philosophical desire for unity which developed at the height of Graeco-Roman culture independently of religious considerations. The other was the increasing need experienced by men to satisfy deep inner demands and conflicts, whereas both fetishism and polytheism ministered mainly to material wants. In fact, he sees monotheism as partly a manifestation of, and partly a response to, an increasing sense of spiritual crisis.

Monotheism eventually provided a combination of reason and faith that was to prove irresistible. Constant attributes its final victory, however, to its sense of the infinite:

Monotheism possesses this undoubted advantage over polytheism that it puts into men's minds an indefinable idea, or perhaps a feeling, of the infinite. This idea, this feeling is more favorable to morality than any fixed, dogmatic and positive doctrine. The absence of limits applied to our feelings and our thoughts tends most to purify the former and elevate the latter. All generous emotions rest on this idea, even when it is unnoticed. Love is ennobled and purified only because, as long as it lasts, it believes that it cannot end.[26]

In short, the value and the advantages of monotheism belong to its fundamental nature; only passing circumstances such as an inadequate expression of its ideals can undermine it—and then only temporarily.

Characteristically, Constant sees intolerance as one such undermining influence, and inevitably he attributes it to the priesthood. Once monotheism is freed from sacerdotal domination, he says, intolerance will vanish. Writing in post-Revolutionary France, he believed he could see signs that the ground was being prepared for the tolerant and gentle religion which was his ideal. It was certainly not Catholicism, but neither was it Genevan Protestantism. It was an individual, largely unorganized religious feeling focussed on a God of goodness and love—benevolent toward his children, moved to pity by their errors, satisfied by the pure intentions, rather than the detailed forms, of their worship. In fact, the religious position which Constant adopted during the last two decades of his life, with its indulgent and individualistic emphases, was of a piece with his general liberalism.

Constant envisaged no radically new development beyond monotheism, but simply an increasing refinement of it. Turning to his own day, he asserted that the theories of the Enlightenment and the practices of the Revolution had left true religion unscathed, destroying only those man-made additions which were, in any case, imperfections: "One witnesses the disappearance of oppressive corporate power, of unjust principles of intolerance, of narrow notions reducing religion to the level of commerce or giving exaggerated importance to detailed practices. The content survived this destruction of external forms and man has again taken an enormous step forward toward the ennoblement of his nature and towards his eternal destiny."[27]

CHAPTER 6

Literary Theory

I N Chapter 4, on the subject of press freedom, we found
Constant implying that in any conflict between the freedom
of an individual citizen and the general health of a national
literature his sympathies would be with the former rather than
the latter. This is one of many pieces of evidence suggesting
that he regarded political action (and religious speculation
also) as more important activities than the practice of the arts.
In the same vein, in the course of a letter to Mme de Charrière
dated 7 June 1794, he praised German philosophy and historiog-
raphy, but offered to make her a free gift of all Germany's poets
(tragic, comic, and lyrical), and added firmly: "I do not like
poetry in any language." [1]

We know, of course, that Constant had the usual literary ambitions of an intelligent and sensitive small boy (he wrote *Les
Chevaliers* at the age of twelve), and his dislike of poetry did
not prevent him from writing *Le Siège de Soissons* and publishing *Wallstein*, an adaptation of Schiller's trilogy *Wallenstein*, in
1809. Although it is tempting to see him as a paradoxical figure—
as one who scorned literature yet displayed, almost casually, outstanding literary gifts in at least one work—this would be a false
picture. In fact, he was prompted by a measure of literary ambition in the writing of *Le Cahier rouge* and *Cécile*, as well as in
his masterpiece *Adolphe*, and as the years passed he became
something of a theorist of literature as well as a practitioner.
While some of his theoretical writings are of particular literary-
historical interest because they contain, partly under the influence
of Mme de Staël, a distinctive early-Romantic emphasis, many
of his ideas are grounded in an approach to literature as a social
and cultural phenomenon. These ideas were shaped above all
by political considerations and his everpresent concern with
freedom.

I *Literature as a Social Phenomenon*

Constant's views on the social status and role of literature, views which received scattered expression at various points in his life, are conveniently (if somewhat contradictorily) expressed in an essay, "De la littérature dans ses rapports avec la liberté," included in the *Mélanges de littérature et de politique* of 1829. The title of the essay is identical with that of a chapter in Mme de Staël's *De l'Allemagne* of 1810, and the main ideas also recall her *De la littérature considérée dans ses rapports avec les institutions sociales* of 1800. Nevertheless, Constant imposes his own distinctive form of argument on his essay and gives it an historical dimension lacking in Mme de Staël's writings.

The main approach in "De la littérature dans ses rapports avec la liberté" is colored by the need to consider, and in some cases to refute, certain arguments current at the time among those whom Constant regarded as his political opponents. These opponents, in the course of making a counterrevolutionary case for authority and control, had often argued that literature in France significantly reached a peak of excellence under the absolutist reign of Louis XIV. Gradually, however, in the aftermath of the Revolution, their arguments began to change. Thirty years after the fall of the Bastille, they were claiming freedom to be an important theme in seventeenth-century literature. The eighteenth-century *philosophes*, they insisted, were not the first proponents of liberty or the first opponents of despotism. An authentic, nonrevolutionary concept of freedom is to be found in such theocratic writers as Massillon, Bourdaloue, and even Bossuet. Such are the claims which Constant set out to examine further, and from which he tried to derive some general principles.

He remarks that this *volte-face* on the part of his opponents is itself testimony to the fundamental power of ideas of liberty and freedom. Furthermore, on the grounds that their arguments are less powerful than they might be because partisanship always narrows horizons, he proposes to add other arguments to their case. He begins by establishing the general point that a concern with freedom on the part of a writer is rarely a reflection of an existing state of social and political liberty. On the contrary, literature usually stands in a dialectical relationship to the social conditions under which it is written. He goes further and claims that a writer may be a true lover of freedom and yet accept despotic institutions through ignorance of the nature and possibilities of political liberty. By the same token, post-Revolutionary France has clearly shown that by no means all partisans of political liberty are genuine lovers of freedom. In fact, Constant is rightly concerned to reject any falsely simplified one-to-one relationship between social organization and literary expression.

Having made these general points, Constant goes on to examine, in particular, the Augustan age in Roman literature. Rather like the age of Louis XIV in France, the age of Augustus (dating from 44 B.C. to A.D. 17) was one of outstanding literary and artistic achievement. What Constant establishes as a false argument, however, is one which in either case seeks to demonstrate a direct relationship between artistic achievement and political and social despotism. Nevertheless, although literary excellence makes no case for authoritarian rule any more than political freedom guarantees artistic quality, Constant believes that progress in literature—the creation of new forms and the communication of new ideas and experiences—is somehow linked with a concern for freedom on the part of men of letters: ". . . progress in literature, however much one likes to conceive of it as being separate from all political considerations, and although no doubt unconnected with an explicit and guaranteed form of liberty, is always related to a movement in the minds of men which has something to do with liberty as memory, possession or desire—in a word, with their sense of freedom." [2]

Having formulated this conviction, Constant has some difficulty in relating it satisfactorily to the historical facts and circumstances of Roman literature. He argues that the greatest literary figures of the period, although living under despotism, came to maturity in a time of relative liberty. Major exceptions, he admits, are Horace, Ovid, and Virgil. Although few, if any, writers under Augustus were as outspoken as Catullus in their opposition to despotism, their flattery of their rulers or patrons could not wholly conceal an underlying concern for freedom.

This kind of argument suggests that Constant is making the best of a bad job. His position is further weakened by having to make exceptions of such outstanding names as Horace and Virgil. It is clear that his evaluation of Roman literature is excessively influenced at this stage by political considerations, or at least by his central preoccupation with freedom. He makes considerable efforts, of course, to show that Horace and Virgil owed the perfection of their art not to social discipline, but to nostalgia for freedom, which proved to be the source of what is most beautiful and most profound in their writings. There is an element of circularity in this argument, however, since he identifies beauty and profoundity with a concern for liberty in the first place.

Turning to the post-Augustan era, Constant relates the decadence of Roman literature to the effect of slavery both on the *âmes vulgaires* and on the *petit nombre d'âmes encore profondes et élevées*. He does not explain or analyse the nature of this alleged effect of slavery on both the common people and an intellectual élite, apart from discerning in the literature of the period an emphatic and exaggerated tone which he attributes to the indignation which slavery aroused in certain writers. The authors whom he quotes as examples are Lucan, Seneca, Persius, and Juvenal. Their exaggerated style reflected the decadence of their times. Their strong feeling for stoicism shows that this doctrine provided a refuge and oblique means of expression for their love of liberty.

At the end of his essay, Constant reverts, even more directly, to the one-to-one relationship which he argued against earlier. He identifies an increase of freedom under Trajan with the literary and intellectual distinction of Quintilian and Tacitus. On the same basis, he ends with the statement that when freedom was suppressed yet again, literature expired (with the younger Pliny). It is worth adding that, although Constant limited himself to Latin examples in this essay, the manuscripts in the Bibliothèque Nationale collection include the outline of a much more extended treatment. This would have dealt with the age of Louis XIV as well as with that of Augustus, and there would have been chapters on English and German literature.

II *Literary Judgments*

We know that Constant was raised on a diet of the Greek and Latin classics, together with the major writers of seventeenth and eighteenth-century France. Later, he read the eighteenth-century *philosophes* more systematically—particularly Voltaire,

Rousseau, and Montesquieu—and he also extended his knowledge of German and English literature. His comments on his reading, particularly in his early years, are scattered through his correspondence and scarcely amount to a coherent critical position. However, in his *Journal* and in various letters of the early 1800's, he made a number of literary judgments which are of interest because of the light they throw on his own tastes and ideas. Also, they anticipate in several ways the theories he was to set out, in the last years of his life, in such writings as the revised preface to *Wallstein*, two articles on the nature of tragedy, and several essays published in the *Mélanges de littérature et de politique*.

It is clear that by the turn of the century Constant was critical of the dominant French literary tradition, particularly in drama. For example, in the *Journal* for 30 March 1804,[3] he expresses his enthusiastic admiration for Sophocles, but then states that the limits of what is permissible are too narrowly drawn in the French theatre. At the same time, he admits that these limits are necessary since the French instinct for attracting attention by making a splash would otherwise lead dramatists to extravagance and bad taste. The logical outcome of these two statements would seem to be an admiration for foreign rather than French dramatists. This was Constant's general position. In the Greek theatre, however, he appreciated dramatists of very different skills. He praises the unity, restraint, and tragic inevitability that characterize the plays of Sophocles, but this does not prevent him from responding to the theatre of Euripides. It is true that the latter's tragedies are less unified than those of Sophocles and do not possess the same powerful tragic inevitability. Nevertheless, the combination in Euripides of bitter irony and heartrending sensibility compels his admiration. In a further *Journal* entry for the following month, he expresses his characteristically politico-moral approach to imaginative writing. He presents Euripides as a man whose thwarted ambition turned into hatred of democracy and who could have written Voltaire's *Tancrède*, including the line—"so ridiculous in its context"— "Injustice in the end creates independence."

Among other non-French writers, Constant met and admired both Goethe and Schiller. It is true that the *Journal* for the early 1800's contains adverse criticism of plays by both dramatists (though there is also praise for Schiller's *Wilhelm Tell*), but

Constant, surprisingly enough, responded to the original nature of their poetry. He described it as poetry of suggestion and evocation, rather than poetry of definition,[4] and regarded it as more truly poetic than the versifying of French neoclassicism:

Difficulty of making German poetry acceptable to a mind accustomed to French poetry. French poetry always has an aim other than that of poetic beauty. It is a matter of morals or utility or experience or finesse or banter, in a word it is always a question of conscious thought. As a result, the poetic has no role in it except as a vehicle or as a means. There is not that impression, that yielding to spontaneous feelings, that description which is so natural and so prompted by impulse that the author does not seem to be aware that he is describing; in short, there is an absence of what characterizes German poetry and what, since I have come to know it, seems to me to be the essence of true poetry. The Frenchman and the Englishman say to you: "Look at the way I describe objects." The German: "This is how objects strike me." . . . But the result is that people accustomed to looking in poetry for things other than the poetic do not find what they seek in German poetry. Like the mathematician who said of *Iphigenia* "What does it prove?" foreigners say of German poetry: "Where does it lead?" [5]

It should be noted that Constant wrote this entry in his *Journal* in 1804, sixteen years before the publication of Lamartine's *Méditations poétiques.* It is an interesting yet little-known anticipation of what was to become, in general terms, the Romantic conception of poetry.

At the same time Constant was not always generous, or gifted with insight, in his comments on those of his contemporaries whose writings also anticipated later Romantic developments. For example, it is true that he spoke of Chateaubriand as the leading French writer of his age and regarded *René* as one of the finest works in the French language. Nevertheless, he also claimed that the style of *Les Martyrs,* through being so high-flown, was boring and sleep-inducing. As for *René,* his favorable judgment is followed by the malicious remark: "Besides, Chateaubriand put so little reason, or rather so much folly, into the rest of his five volumes [of *Le Génie du christianisme*] that it is not surprising to find that, wanting to be reasonable for once, he discovered a great deal of common sense at his disposal." [6] In fact, Constant's general opinion (largely justified in itself, but somewhat surprising in view of other statements) is that Chateaubriand was too free with emotion and too sparing of rationality.

The one pre-Romantic contemporary whom Constant praised enthusiastically was, as might be expected, Mme de Staël. The essence of his views can be found in "De Madame de Staël et de ses ouvrages," one of the essays in *Mélanges de littérature et de politique*. The most interesting aspect of these views is the element of general theory included in their formulation. For example, Constant claimed that *Corinne* was an outstanding artistic achievement, but in doing so he indicated what he thought the essential elements of a successful literary work to be. He also suggested certain criteria by which criticism and literary judgment should be guided.

As regards characterization, he repeatedly stresses the need for the reader to grant certain concessions to the author. He argues that a writer must be free to create fictional figures designed to serve his own particular purposes. Corinne, for example, is given certain characteristics because Mme de Staël uses her as part of a wider portrayal of Italy and Italian life. This purpose makes for a certain idealization and stylization in character portrayal, but this is a normal, and often admirable, quality of art. Some characters are unconvincing because of inconsistencies in their conception or inadequacies in their presentation. Others have convincing features raised beyond the merely human to a certain level of intensity and aesthetic perfection achieved by literary skill. Constant criticizes the first kind of characterization, but praises the latter. The questions he asks of fictional heroes or heroines are: Are they coherently portrayed by the author? Do they move us? Are the circumstances and actions through which they are presented consistent with their character? Do we follow their emotions and actions with increasing interest as the novel (or play) progresses? He concludes that if we can answer these questions in the affirmative, the work under discussion is close to perfection.[7] His ideal might be expressed as an artistically perfected consistency in the service of a greater understanding of human beings.

Apart from characterization, the other main theoretical question discussed in this essay is the moral status of a literary work. Constant makes it quite clear that he regards an obtrusive "lesson" in a work of art (he instances the fables of La Fontaine) as a considerable blemish. He argues that an explicit moral aim tends to undermine the power of character, circumstance, and action to convince us in purely human terms. He neatly sums up his position when he writes: "A work of the imagination must not have a moral goal, but a moral effect. In this respect it must resemble human life which does not have a goal, yet which always produces an effect in which morality necessarily plays a part." [8] If, as a result of reading an imaginative work, the more kindly, generous, or noble aspects of our nature have been roused, then the work is "moral" in the best sense. The distinction is a familiar one between the moral and the moralistic.

As we have seen already, Constant is also responsive to the moral effect of beauty and aesthetic perfection. This is a view which he again underlines here. While he acknowledges the ethical effect of content (the moving revelation of human problems and qualities through character and action), he also makes a special case for the moral impact of form.

III Classical and Romantic Theatre

The German poet and dramatist, Friedrich Schiller, displayed a passionate concern with freedom in much of his work. Given Constant's similar preoccupations, it is not surprising that he wanted to make Schiller's writings better known in France. In September, 1807, he began work on a French adaptation of the German dramatist's trilogy, *Wallenstein,* which had appeared in 1798–99. He gave the title *Wallstein* to this version of Schiller's work, wrote a preface entitled "Quelques réflexions sur la tragédie de *Wallstein* et sur le théâtre allemand," and published both play and preface in 1809.

Constant thought highly of his play, regarding certain scenes as outstandingly good.[9] The main purpose of the preface was to justify his departures from Schiller's text and to explain and defend, to the French public, the unfamiliar conception of drama behind Schiller's trilogy. In fact, however, the play was not performed and was the object of a good deal of adverse criticism. Constant's preface failed to win over the critics, he gradually came himself to accept a number of their objections, and a revised version of the preface—an essay published twenty years later in *Mélanges de littérature et de politique*—includes some interesting remarks on why his adaptation of Schiller proved a failure.

In the 1809 preface, Constant had begun by emphasizing the difficulty, and defending the necessity, of adapting Schiller's trilogy as a single play. In the 1829 essay, he indicates the different expectations of German theatre audiences by stating that the three parts of *Wallenstein* are sometimes produced separately in Germany. Thus *Wallensteins Lager*, on its own, becomes a play devoid of action; *Die Piccolomini* provides action but no *dénouement*; *Wallensteins Tod* amounts to a play with a *dénouement* but lacking an exposition. All this implies a freedom in the German theatre which is foreign to French audiences. Constant sees it as one of his mistakes that he tried to adapt Schiller's subject to the relatively restrictive rules of French neoclassical drama. Later he explains this point further by saying that the French portray a fact or a passion in their plays whereas the Germans sketch out a whole life or a complete character. Racine's plays are offered as examples of this dominant French tradition. Racine, Constant says, tells us nothing, for example, about Phèdre's character apart from her passion for Hippolyte. He adds: "By only portraying a passion instead of embracing a complete individual character, one obtains more consistently tragic effects because individual characters, which are always mixed, harm the unity of these effects. But perhaps truth is harmed even more. . . . Besides, there is much less variety in the passions deemed appropriate to tragedy than in individual characters as created by nature. There are countless characters, but a very limited number of theatrical passions." [10]

On a different though related point, Constant claims that French readers proved unsympathetic to the element of superstition in Wallenstein's character. More generally, they were insensitive to the sense of mystery in Schiller's portrayal of his hero. Then follows another passage which is again, in effect, an anticipation of the Romantic attitude to human experience. This is the approach to life which Schiller conveyed. Constant sympathized with it, but found it impossible to express convincingly within the limits of the traditional rules of French drama.[11] He did not possess the literary originality which would have enabled him to break the Classical mold in such a way as to give the new sensibility satisfactory artistic form.

Constant has interesting things to say about other features of his adaptation. By following the tendency of his German model to vary the linguistic tone of the trilogy and introduce passages of familiar speech, he departed from the unity of tone and the *pompe poétique* to which the French ear is accustomed. Again, by reducing the number of characters from forty-eight to twelve, in an attempt to approach more closely to French practice, he lost the whole dimension of the secondary characters which was important in the German drama and virtually non-existent in the French. Thirdly, in order to respect the French Classical conventions, he found it necessary to use the relatively artificial device of the *récit*, whereas the German original had put a number of the events thus described directly on the stage. Lastly, because of a fundamental difference between the French and German conceptions of love (animal in the case of the French and mystical in the case of the Germans),[12] Schiller's heroine Thekla was neither properly understood nor easily accepted by French readers.

One of the most interesting aspects of these four points is that Constant, in making them, was criticizing some of the central dramatic traditions which the Romantic theorists also attacked. He was writing his essay two years after Hugo's preface to *Cromwell* (1827), and there are distinct similarities between the two documents. He was particularly concerned, of course, to account for his own failure. At first he appears to be doing so by blaming French conventionalism rather than his own artistic shortcomings, but in fact he shows considerable insight into his own misjudgment of the changing literary ideas of his contemporaries. He admits, in effect, that he was adapting Schiller's play to a set of conventions which, as early as 1809, were already being modified. He should have foreseen, he says, that political and social revolution would eventually be followed by a corresponding upheaval in literary sensibility. He was deceived in part by the surface immobility of society and literature under the Empire. Also, some of the most zealous early revolutionary figures were as conservative in their artistic tastes as they were violent in their political views. Classical Roman ideals of discipline and restraint were much prized in the art and thought of Revolutionary and post-Revolutionary France. Constant goes so far as to assert that all writers during the

Empire were Classical in outlook and practice. He does not exclude Marie-Joseph Chénier (brother of the more famous André), whose verse tragedy *Charles IX* had strong pro-Revolution implications when it was produced in 1789. He points out that, on the artistic level, even Chénier was a keen defender of the literary restrictions "bequeathed by Aristotle and consecrated by Boileau."

In view of these facts, one may think that Constant was unduly self-critical about his failure, in 1809, to anticipate changes of attitude and theory which, particularly in the theatre, did not receive explicit and well-publicized formulation until the late 1820's. Unless he had been a dramatist of outstanding originality and talent (which he clearly was not), he could not have achieved in 1809 what had become a widely defined ideal by 1829. He is not afraid to say, however, that the "liberation" of the theatre has led to excesses. Some dramatists, having rightly broken free from the Classical rules, have been too concerned to create a powerful effect at all costs. He sees clearly that, as a result, the Romantic drama has too often turned its back on reality, naturalness, and good taste.[13] Nevertheless, the essay ends with some clear criticisms of the unities of time and place and of the awkwardness and even absurdity to which they can give rise. Although excessive changes of scene in a play can admittedly lead to confusion and formlessness, Constant makes it clear in the final paragraph that, given an ultimate framework of order, he is at heart a partisan of freedom in the sphere of literature as well as in politics and religion.

IV *Tragedy and Social Reality*

The last substantial piece of literary theorizing by Constant consisted of two articles, under the general title "Réflexions sur la tragédie," originally published in the *Revue de Paris* of 1829. Significantly enough, particularly in view of his earlier attitude to literature, he wrote these two articles, in part at least, as a form of relief from pressing political problems.

Early in the first article, Constant distinguishes three types of tragedy. The first, especially familiar in France, is mainly concerned with the portrayal of one particular passion. Examples would include such plays as Racine's *Phèdre* and *Andromaque*, or Voltaire's *Mérope*. In the second type of tragedy, the study of character in much wider terms is the overriding consideration. Constant instances *Hamlet, Richard III,* and various plays by Goethe and Schiller. He also detects the germ of "character" tragedy in Racine's *Britannicus* and in several of Voltaire's plays. In the third type of tragedy, the central theme is one of conflict between an individual and certain social forces by which he is surrounded. No play, to Constant's knowledge, fully meets his criteria for this type of tragedy, but it is the form which he believes tragedy should take in the future. So far, the action of society has been given a subsidiary role in tragedy, providing, at best, a setting or framework for the study of passion or character. Whether their setting is historical or contemporary, tragedies should now have as their active, central element the impact of social forces on individuals.

Before going on to explain and argue these ideas more fully, Constant makes a number of criticisms of the first two types of tragedy. As regards the "theatre of passion," he notes that the passion in question is almost always love, and suggests that this particular mine is now becoming worked out. Furthermore, love is a less popular subject for literary treatment (he claims) in a society in which access to women has been made much easier and in which other activities, including politics, increasingly absorb men's attention. The suggestion is made that Voltaire's "philosophical" tragedies were born in part out of a realization of this fact, though in some cases they are spoiled as tragedies by the partisan spirit which pervades them. In fact, however, Voltaire receives more praise from Constant than does Racine. For example, the latter's *Phèdre,* although described as the most perfect of French tragedies belonging to the *genre passionné,* is criticized on the grounds that it fails to teach any moral precepts designed to "improve" the spectators. This is a surprising line of argument—the more so since it implies that very moralistic criterion of literary excellence which Constant was concerned to refute in some of his earlier writings.

As regards characters, he thinks that they are no more inexhaustible a source of dramatic material than is the passion of love. Where a tragedy does depend on character portrayal, the character in question must be both consistent and outstanding. Characters in the tragic theatre must, indeed, be presented with a heightened intensity which sets them above the ordinary.

"When we go to the theatre," he writes, "we wish to see people greater than our friends." [14] On these grounds, he argues that Félix, in Corneille's *Polyeucte*, is portrayed *realistically* in his incoherence, but is not a *tragic* figure.

This last point raises some difficulty since Constant earlier criticized Racine for avoiding such incoherence by concentrating exclusively on a single passion (for example, in the case of Phèdre). In fact, Constant is aware of the dilemma which arises and which he formulates as a choice between "suppressing, in the case of the characters, everything which fails to contribute to the action and, all the more, anything which runs counter to it . . . or retaining individual characteristics at the risk of destroying unity and disconcerting the audience." [15] It is a choice, he adds, between renouncing truth or sacrificing dramatic interest.

Constant's conclusion is that neither passion nor character can provide a satisfactory focus for tragedy in the theatre. Even if he sees, in Voltaire's play *Mahomet*, an ideal combination of passion and character, he regards this as an outstanding exception and claims that both passion and character are subsidiary to the action of society on individuals. Such a view may cause problems for his doctrine of individual freedom, but it is certainly in keeping with several of his other ideas and activities. He asserts that "this action of society is the most important factor in human life." [16] Everything starts from, and ends in, social reality and social pressure. He believes that it is no longer possible to construct a tragedy around the Greek concept of fatality. It is important, in fact, that tragedy should be used to fix the spectators' attention on the crucial role played by society in individual lives.

It is curious that a person as notably self-divided as Constant should have seen tragedy as something arising from conflict between the individual and society rather than from contrasting elements within the individual himself. However, although this was his position as far as the theatre is concerned, we shall see in the next chapter that in his novel, *Adolphe*, self-division is a central feature and a major (though not exclusive) source of Adolphe's tragic experience.

As regards the two articles now under discussion, Constant goes on to provide examples of what he considers to be suitable social material for tragedy. At a general level, he instances political oppression or religious persecution, and he also quotes, in detail, an incident of royal vengeance on the part of Louis XIV recounted in Saint-Simon's *Mémoires*. He regards the action of society as the modern counterpart of Classical fatality; tragedy and fatality have become social, even societal, in essence.

It has to be said that most of Constant's proposed subjects for modern tragedy, and the way in which he advocates them, sound quite disastrous as recipes for theatrical success. Nevertheless, he expresses a great deal of enthusiasm for this new theatre of social reality and social pressure. Indeed, he finds it aesthetically liberating as well as politically and humanly relevant. These are plays in which the unities of time and place not only can, but must, be dispensed with. He also has some interesting things to say, in passing, about the importance of local color (geographical and historical) in the type of tragedy which he advocates. He points out, incidentally, the importance of such local color in the writings of the historians of his own day—Guizot, Barante, Thierry, etc.—in contrast to the earlier generation of Hume, Robertson, and Gibbon. Finally, he discusses a German play, *Die Macht der Verhältnisse*, by Louis Robert. Despite finding some faults and difficulties in it, he praises the author for his decision not to portray a hero, but the powerful part played by rank and position within the graduated levels of an essentially hierarchical society.

CHAPTER 7

Cécile *and* Adolphe

U NTIL the early 1950's, Constant's very considerable literary
reputation was almost exclusively based on his hundred-
page novel *Adolphe*. It had always been known that he had
written another work of fiction, *Cécile*, but its character was
unclear and the manuscript presumed lost. It was therefore a
dramatic moment in the history of Constant studies when a
copy of the lost manuscript turned up unexpectedly in a collection of family papers as recently as 1948. The text was edited
and published by the distinguished Constant scholar, Alfred
Roulin, in 1951.

Cécile was never completed by Constant. He appears to have
mislaid it among the documents which he left in Göttingen after
his stay there in 1813. Nevertheless, seven of the eight projected
époques or precisely dated chapters were written, containing a
fictionalized account of his relationship with Charlotte von Hardenberg over fifteen years (1793 to 1808), and culminating in a
painful analysis of his vacillation between the relatively unde-
manding love of Charlotte and the imperious domination of Mme
de Staël. Because of the inherent interest and quality of the novel,
Constant's literary reputation could now be given a broader base.
Furthermore, the discovery of *Cécile*—and a reading of Alfred
Roulin and Charles Roth's definitive text of the *Journaux intimes*
in conjunction with the novel—shed new light on the origins of
Adolphe. The result was a reexamination of previous critical
assumptions concerning the scope and purpose of *Adolphe*. In
fact, before discussing each work separately and in detail, it is
necessary to attempt a brief account of the interrelated origins
of the two novels.

I *A Double Genesis*

Both *Cécile* and *Adolphe* take their origin from two circumstances which arose in October, 1806: Constant was feeling

particularly restive under the demanding régime imposed by Mme de Staël, and he had fallen in love with Charlotte von Hardenberg. He had first met the latter thirteen years previously at the Brunswick court where her husband, Baron Marenholz, occupied an official position as chamberlain. They met again in 1804 and exchanged some letters subsequently. At this time Charlotte was Mme Dutertre, having divorced her first husband and married a French *émigré* in 1798. Their further meeting in 1806 was crucial, and Constant found himself caught in an acute moral and emotional dilemma.

The first indication of his intention to transpose his experience into fictional form occurs in the *Journal* for 30 October 1806 where he notes: "Begun a novel which will tell our story." [1] It seems from this that his original idea was to write the story of his love for Charlotte in terms of the eventual triumph of true feeling over a series of personal and social vicissitudes.

It is impossible to say precisely what followed because of the scattered, and sometimes enigmatic or ambiguous, evidence in the *Journal* and letters. Various critics [2] have offered their own interpretation of this evidence, but something of the confusion inherent in the situation may be gathered from the fact that there is no agreement on the identity of the "novel" referred to in the 30 October entry. Roulin and Paul Bénichou tend to identify it with *Adolphe*, and argue that the latter novel was virtually complete and in its final form by the end of 1806. J.-H. Bornecque, Pierre Deguise and Andrew Oliver, on the other hand, identify the "novel" with *Cécile*, while Anthony Pugh argues ingeniously for the existence of a third novel of 1806 which is neither *Cécile* nor *Adolphe*.

What these conflicting interpretations do imply, however, is some kind of link, in their original conception, between the two works. It is clear that Constant began to write a novel in 1806, whether *Cécile* or not, which would recount the story of his long, often interrupted, relationship with Charlotte. However, by 4 November, we find him noting the need to "change the form" of his novel. Whatever the reasons for this change, he refers in several entries from 10 November onward to work on an "episode concerning Ellénore," and expresses doubt concerning his ability to complete the (original) novel. There is also a note about the advisability or not of publishing the "episode" separ-

Cécile and Adolphe

ately from the "novel." Later, however, he refers several times
to working on his "novel" again, and a note of 21 December,
which indicates that the death of Ellénore is an important scene
in this novel, suggests that the earlier "episode" had now taken
on the form and status of a novel and developed into an early
version of *Adolphe*. A week later, reporting in his *Journal* that
he had read this novel to M. de Boufflers, he adds: "The meaning
of the novel was thoroughly grasped. It is true that I have not
written out of the imagination. *Non ignara mali*. This reading
has demonstrated to me that the work would come to nothing
if I included another feminine episode. (The hero would be
repulsive.) Ellénore would cease to be interesting and, if the
hero took on obligations toward another woman yet failed to
fulfill them, his weakness would become odious."[3]

At least two important conclusions can be drawn from this
passage. Firstly, the Ellénore episode, now become a novel in
its own right, began with the idea (inherent in the 1806 situation) of presenting the hero as torn between two women but
ended, for moral and artistic reasons, by concentrating on his
relationship with Ellénore and removing irrelevant secondary
themes. Furthermore, this relationship was linked directly with
the most difficult half of Constant's immediate problem—his
inability to disengage himself from a woman (Mme de Staël/
Ellénore) with whom he had contracted deep and long-estab-
lished links. On 31 December 1806 he notes the criticism that the
illness of Ellénore is brought about too abruptly in the novel, and
with this in mind he worked at it further. It seems reasonable to
conclude that *Adolphe* as we now know it was completed, apart
from some late and probably minor revisions, in 1807.

It cannot be conclusively proved, of course, that the identification of "episode" and "novel" made in the argument above is
wholly justified. It has been argued that the "episode" is the
nascent *Adolphe*, the "novel" the embryonic *Cécile*, and that
Constant worked at both concurrently. The *Journal* entries make
it difficult to accept this interpretation, but the question remains
regarding what happened to the initial project of 1806 centered
on Charlotte. It is possible that some kind of initial outline of
Cécile was sketched during November, 1806 (Anthony Pugh is
tempted to call it *Charlotte*, not *Cécile*), but it seems to have
been dropped by Constant in favor of his "episode" centered on

Ellénore. He certainly did not write the version of *Cécile* which we now have earlier than 1809 or later than 1812, and there is force in Roulin's hypothesis that the project was taken up again, with or without a backward glance at a manuscript of 1806, towards the end of 1811.[4] This view is strengthened by the fact that *Cécile* does not appear among the inventory of his works which Constant drew up in the summer of 1810. It is clear from a reading of the text that *Cécile* is much closer than *Adolphe* to the original project of 1806, though *Adolphe* also grew out of—and away from—the 1806 situation as we have seen. *Cécile* describes a hero torn by his different obligations to two contrasting women—something which Constant was unable to transpose satisfactorily into fictional form in 1806 while he was living this dilemma intensely, but which he succeeded in conveying with considerable skill in 1811 at a moment when he had finally broken with Mme de Staël and was still content in his marriage to Charlotte. To this extent *Cécile* can be viewed as offering, at least in original intention, an ultimately happy sequel to the personal tribulations transposed into fictional form in *Adolphe*. The general narrative framework of *Cécile* is more specifically autobiographical than that of *Adolphe*, though both works contain different degrees of stylization of personal experience.

II *Fact and Fiction in* Cécile

It may seem odd to discuss *Cécile* before *Adolphe* since it was completed later and extends to a later period in Constant's life. Nevertheless, it represents the fulfillment of literary intentions which preceded the writing of *Adolphe*, and it is also unfinished and a less fully realized work of art. If it succeeds *Adolphe* in terms of composition, it antedates it in terms of literary achievement. In these circumstances it seems right that this study should end with an analysis of *Adolphe*, which remains Constant's masterpiece and his best-known work.

On its first appearance in 1951, *Cécile* was interpreted by a number of scholars as a piece of thinly disguised and fundamentally reliable autobiography.[5] Given the period which the novel spans—11 January 1793 to 2 February 1808—it was welcomed as filling a previously irritating gap in Constant's *Journaux intimes* and seen as a pendant to the *Cahier rouge*. To give Charlotte von Hardenberg the fictional name of Cécile de Walterbourg and Mme de Staël that of Mme de Malbée hardly concealed the fact that Constant was working with the basic elements of his own personal situation. Furthermore, certain precise geographical locations—Brunswick, Paris, Lausanne, etc.—and the dates of certain journeys and other happenings, coincided with a number of established facts in the Constant biography. Nevertheless, the almost exclusively autobiographical interpretation could not be sustained for very long. *Cécile* was clearly intended as a work of fiction, however much it might draw initially on fact. Despite the precise dating of the seven *époques*, it was also clear that some liberties had been taken with the real-life chronology. Again, the fact that fictional names were used, in contrast to the *Journal* and *Cahier rouge*, suggested a somewhat different conception and purpose. It can still be argued, sensibly enough, that *Cécile* is more a stylized autobiography than a fully rounded novel, but the considerable extent of this stylization, indulged in chiefly for aesthetic reasons, has only become very clear comparatively recently.

Constant's departures from strict autobiography are of three main kinds. He altered most of the real-life characters on which he drew in the course of transforming them into fictional figures. He modified certain events. He introduced themes and episodes derived from an existing literary tradition rather than from precise personal experience.

If we turn first to alterations of character, we may note that Andrew Oliver has shown the considerable gap that exists between Charlotte and Cécile.[6] Inevitably, the Charlotte/Cécile of 1811 differs from the actual Charlotte of, for example, 1793. But apart from the distorting effect of time, and the idealization encouraged by Constant's renewed love for Charlotte from 1804 onward, artistic considerations also enter in. It is necessary, for the balance and drama of the novel, that Cécile should be an *ange de douceur*—an angelic and long-suffering creature who is the temperamental opposite of Mme de Malbée. Therefore, as Oliver points out, Constant suppresses, in the novel, his quick tiring of Charlotte in 1793; there is no word of the mediocrity and stupidity of which he complained to Mme de Charrière. There is evidence, too, that the real Charlotte was rather less perfect than the fictional Cécile, but this would have proved an awkward element in the rather stylized contrast between the two heroines (or rather, heroine and antiheroine). With much the same considerations in mind, he is particularly severe on Cécile's two husbands in the novel making them more unrelievedly unsympathetic than their real life models appear to have been.

As regards Mme de Malbée, Simone Balayé has demonstrated that she is something less than a true portrayal of Mme de Staël.[7] If Constant strayed from the facts in his fictional highlighting of Charlotte/Cécile's virtues, he also departed from strict truth in some of his cutting remarks concerning Mme de Staël/Mme de Malbée's faults. Typical of his barbed comments in the novel is his observation on Mme de Malbée's grief at her father's death: "Mme de Malbée, who is sincere in her suffering, but who found her suffering an inconvenience, wished to find distraction in Italy."[8] The third *époque* is largely taken up with a portrait of Mme de Malbée. She is presented as a woman possessing a series of carefully balanced attractive and repulsive features. While much of this may well have been true of the real Mme de Staël, the narrator's picture of Mme de Malbée is a very different one from that of Mme de Staël conveyed by Constant in the letters he wrote on first meeting her. It is also in keeping with Constant's stylization that Cécile should have "an exceptionally white skin," "superb arms," and "a gentle voice," whereas Mme de Malbée suffers from "an unpleasant complexion," "rather too large hands," and "an excessively masculine manner." As part of the same approach, and in his account of his experiences with Mme de Malbée, Constant as narrator ignores the considerable help which Constant the politician received from Mme de Staël in 1795 and on the occasion of his nomination to the Tribunate. It is not so much that Constant gives a positively untrue picture of Mme de Staël as that he leaves out many details necessary for a balanced portrait. One feels that by 1811 his motives were not solely literary. He was too close, emotionally, to the final break which had occurred in May of that year to do other than he did. Nevertheless, this was an occasion when his emotional state and his literary purpose coincided very satisfactorily.

As regards the altering of episodes, Professor Frank Bowman has pointed out how much the narrator's account of his contacts with the Quietist sect in Lausanne differs from Constant's own experience.[9] He shows that the novel presents events in a different time sequence from that which they followed in Constant's life; that the doctrine of Quietism, with which Constant was certainly fully familiar, is simplified in a way that suits the particular emotional dilemma experienced by the hero; that he suppresses entirely the religious side of Mme de Staël's temperament in his description of Mme de Malbée, etc. The text of *Cécile* scarcely supports this last assertion, but otherwise these points are well noted and convincingly made. We need to remind ourselves however that these apparent "criticisms" of Constant, both as regards characterization and the plotting of certain episodes, should be taken as nothing more than conscientious recordings of the gap between fact and fiction in *Cécile*. If such a gap did not exist, Constant would be criticized in earnest for not having transformed his material sufficiently boldly in accordance with the demands of art. Indeed, it can be argued that this last criticism needs to be made; that Constant did not go far enough in distancing himself from his material.

Evidence of this distancing taking the more radical form of conscious literary reminiscence is presented by the German commentator Walter Pabst.[10] He argues that Constant gave art precedence over autobiographical fact by inserting a dramatic episode in the seventh *époque* for which we have no evidence in his own life. This is the account of the narrator's journey from Lausanne to Besançon, of his carriage's running out of control and overturning in the snow, and of Cécile's walking through mud and ice, with her maid, to meet him some distance outside Besançon. Pabst goes on to point out that this episode shares at least a dozen details in common with an incident in Mme de Staël's *Delphine* (Part III, letter 8). This, in its turn, is an elaborate variation on Part IV, letter 6 of *La Nouvelle Héloïse*. Literary reminiscence is also present in the fact that Cécile's portrait appears to owe certain features to the Cécile of Mme de Charrière's novel, *Lettres écrites de Lausanne,* and to the eponymous heroine of its sequel, *Caliste*. At the end of his article, Walter Pabst rightly argues that to transform or stylize autobiographical material in the way we have described above is by no means to lack integrity or sincerity. He distinguishes between "personal" and "literary" sincerity, and sees *Cécile* as an example of the latter. We may say, indeed, that Constant's novel is not an instance of direct, autobiographical veracity, but an attempt to explore and reveal the depths of his own personality, while also creating a coherent fictional character, through a conscious application of the resources of literary art. *Cécile* serves to remind us that "art" can be more revealing of truth than "life."

III   *Narrative Self-Revelation in* Cécile

Because of the unnamed narrator's dilemma in *Cécile*, and because of the intensification of this dilemma by the expedient of two contrasting feminine types, he is both the central figure and the only fully realized character—despite the novel's title. It is true that both Cécile and Mme de Malbée are characterized clearly and positively by descriptive phrases, but their own experience of the drama in which they are involved is largely ignored. They are essentially devices for bringing into play the "impossibility" of the narrator's situation, a situation compounded of weakness, genuine scruples, and apparent bad luck. In many ways, the narrator is a psychological copy of Adolphe, and both characters contain a number of temperamental features which we know to have belonged to Constant himself. As Benjamin was the most absorbing person in Constant's life, so the narrator is the most interesting and thoroughly analysed character in Constant's novel. While we are given set descriptions, inevitably external, of Cécile and Mme de Malbée, the narrator is not only described in a number of summarizing phrases and allowed to plead his own case, he also reveals much of himself, sometimes without any comment, in a variety of situations. Cécile and Mme de Malbée are supporting vignettes; the central, full-length portrait is of the narrator.

When the story opens, at the court of Brunswick in 1793, the narrator is twenty-six years old (Constant's own age at that date). Within the first three or four pages, he reveals several of his most characteristic features: a marked interest in women (more erotic than sentimental); a considerable degree of capriciousness (his original, passionate letter to Cécile was written without any genuine feeling for her; her cold reply at once inspired in him a strong infatuation); a tendency to let others make up his mind for him on crucial issues (on the advice of an elderly woman whom he meets, he decides to free himself from his wife). The first of these characteristics is implicit in the remainder of the novel with its account of separation, divorce,

...with two women at once, and an instinctive ...remarriage. As regards the narrator's *homo* ...cs, these show themselves repeatedly. Cécile's ...at they end their relationship, though apparently in keeping with his own desires, immediately prompts him to renew it. Much later, in 1807, the increasing possibility of the longed-for escape from Mme de Malbée's tyranny makes him distinctly less anxious to separate from her: ". . . the approach of my freedom lessened the bitterness of my enslavement." [11] The dualism of his nature, which attracts him to both women, prevents him from behaving consistently toward either. In different ways, and to different degrees, Cécile and Mme de Malbée are both sacrificed to the narrator's vacillation.

It is a short step from this to his essential weakness and his tendency to let others decide his life for him. Early in the novel the narrator explains how his particular attitude encourages other people to give him advice. He also says: "I have never been able to impress others in such a way as to prevent them saying what I should not have heard. All have continually considered it their mission to give me counsel." [12] Later, during one of his early resolutions to end all contact with Cécile, he says of himself: "I thought myself strong because I resisted Cécile. In fact, I was merely yielding to the influence of another woman who, without any particular purpose, and as a mere result of that secret hatred which women have for one another, enjoyed seeing me cause distress and perhaps humiliation to a person whom she did not know." [13]

This weakness of character, and the impressive self-knowledge which accompanies it, find expression in various other ways. The narrator mentions, for example, that the effect of his attempt to take a strong line with his wife found him quite unprepared: "I was so unaccustomed to exercising authority that I remained nonplussed by her obedience." [14] The same characteristics make him hope that if he forgets about something unpleasant or inconvenient it will go away of its own accord. It is typical—and typically honest—that he should say: "I settled easily on the idea that what was distant and unclear might never happen." [15] Not least of all, like many weak people, the narrator sees himself more than once as the hapless victim of fate or destiny.[16] In a similar way, he is sensitive to social opinion, yet intelligent enough to realize that all vices are pardoned, so long as conventions are respected, in the very society he fears. In fac is a society which demands hypocrisy as an earnest of goou breeding.[17]

Two major incidents underline the narrator's moral weakness. He finds among the Quietist community in Lausanne some theological justification for his inability to order his own life. By accepting with enthusiasm the two principles of prayer and renunciation of the will, he shifts responsibility to the deity and says revealingly: "I felt as though the burden of life had been taken from me. . . . I gave up any sort of control of my own life, both in fact and in intention." [18] Again, on the subject of the carriage accident on the way to Besançon, he describes his thoughts as the vehicle careered downhill out of control: "I really thought we would be killed and felt a deep sense of joy. I needed death in order to be free from the uncertainties of life . . ." [19]

IV *Tragedy and Hope in* Cécile

The narrator's weakness, his escapism, and his sharp intelligence combine to make him indulge in repeated, and mostly successful, equivocation towards both Cécile and Mme de Malbée. It is his weakness, in fact, which determines the main formal mechanism of the novel. This resembles the movement of two pendulums. He continually moves backward and forward in his emotional attitude to each woman, and from side to side as he periodically transfers his loyalty (and presence) from one to the other. He sees clearly that this double vacillation must give rise to charges of deception and bad faith but he himself, again refusing responsibility, regards it as fated.[20] To this extent, the novel amounts to a tragedy of indecision. It is the story of a man unable to make a final choice between two "inevitable evils," [21] and the tragedy is intensified by the fact that these evils have themselves been created by his own irresolution.

It seems clear, nevertheless, that it was not Constant's intention to portray tragic inevitability on the lines of *Adolphe*. The events in *Cécile* are recounted in retrospect at a time when Cécile and the narrator are finally and happily married. Although the narrating and narrated selves are one and the same person, the gap in time which their coexistence involves is of major

importance. Although the narrator shows us the tragic potentialities of his particular dilemma, and more particularly the suffering inflicted on Cécile by his fundamental weakness, the last
words of the opening sentence—". . . Cécile de Walterbourg,
who is now my wife"—are a guarantee of an eventual happy
outcome. At several other points in the novel the narrator reminds
us of his status at the time of writing and conveys the impression
of a wiser and more balanced person looking back over the faults
and weaknesses of a now dead past.

One result of this double narrative viewpoint is that it adds
interest, and even a certain tension, to the unfolding of the story.
Constant takes his epigraph, "Italiam, Italiam," from Book III
of Virgil's *Aeneid*. This is significant as suggesting that the
narrator and Cécile are destined, after great problems and many
vicissitudes, to reach the promised land of happy, married love
rather as Aeneas fulfills his destiny, despite many wanderings
and obstacles, by arriving in Italy and founding Rome. Given
the narrator's fundamental character and the acute difficulties
which it creates for him, the tension lies in the gradual unfolding
of how he finally attained his goal, experienced contentment
and learned wisdom.

Nevertheless, the closer one reads the novel the less convinced
one is that such wisdom and contentment are humanly attainable where this particular narrator is concerned. It is here that
the incomplete state of *Cécile* takes on special importance. Various explanations have been offered for Constant's failure to finish
it, including the suggestion that his deteriorating relations with
his wife after 1811 made the originally intended happy ending
impossible. A more likely explanation would be that he had
created, in the person of his fictional narrator, a character who
resembled himself in many ways, but was also sufficiently different, and possessed too much tragic potential, to make the originally intended successful outcome aesthetically acceptable. The
logic of art, in short, demanded precedence over the facts of
autobiography. It is significant that at the point at which the
novel ends, Cécile has become seriously ill and there is no hint
of recovery. The artistic problem which the whole situation may
have raised for Constant is well expressed by Professor William
Holdheim: "Does the internal logic of the work really permit
her [Cécile's] recovery, followed by a few more years of suf-

fering and the final union of the lovers? Or was the author, reversing the facts, to bring about his heroine's death, thus duplicating the story of Ellénore in *Adolphe?* Was he to sacrifice truth to fiction or fiction to truth?" [22]

Cécile remains a skillfully told story, though an unfinished one. It has style, intelligence, and well-judged changes of narrative pace between the seven *époques.* At the same time, Constant seems to have been hampered by a stylization of fact which did not put a sufficiently large distance between his fiction and his life. By sticking to the basic elements of his autobiography, while at the same time reducing his three main figures to certain strongly emphasized characteristics for purposes of contrast and balance, he locked them up in a fictional world increasingly removed from his own immediate personal circumstances. He then failed, for one reason or another, to take the boldly imaginative step that would have carried *Cécile* beyond stylized autobiography to independent and self-sufficient creativity. In this sense the novel, despite the talent which it displays, is finally a creative failure.

V Adolphe: *from Autobiography to Fiction*

The fact that *Adolphe* grew out of an "episode" in his originally projected autobiographical "novel" may have helped Constant to overcome the problem which remained unsolved in *Cécile.* That he travelled a considerable distance from autobiographical dependence to creative freedom in *Adolphe* is one of several features which the discovery of *Cécile* has helped to underline. Like *Cécile,* but more markedly and more subtly, *Adolphe* now appears distinctly less autobiographical than was once thought. It is also noticeable in this connection that a number of the *Journal* entries for late 1806, referring to *Adolphe,* are concerned only with questions of form and artistic coherence, not with matters of autobiographical accuracy. It remains true that Constant was a writer who relied heavily on personal circumstances for creative impetus, but he managed on one occasion (in *Adolphe*) to go well beyond autobiographical dependence, yet failed on a second occasion (with *Cécile*). One is tempted to conclude, though for somewhat different reasons from those advanced when only *Adolphe* was available, that Constant, as a writer of novels, carried within him the material and the means for one major work only.

Earlier comments on *Cécile* have already made it clear that even intended autobiography, if it is to reach an acceptable artistic level, must undergo a certain amount of stylization. Yet although this may seem to justify Stendhal's remark that every work of art is "a beautiful lie," the fact remains that the act of stylization itself can reveal a considerable amount about an author. Thus we are not claiming that *Adolphe* is less illuminating on the subject of Constant because it now appears less directly autobiographical than used to be thought. It remains a highly "personal" work, and in it Constant can be seen contending with two particular problems which regularly confront the autobiographically inclined novelist. He apparently resists the temptation to reveal only the creditable aspects of the self and seems to allow his fictional hero to be frank about his shortcomings and inconsistencies (e.g., "I have no desire here to justify myself" [23]). But he also has in mind various considerations of artistic coherence which turn out to be inconsistent with unvarnished self-portrayal. The opening pages, for example, give an expository portrait of Adolphe in which he establishes that his mother died in giving him birth, that his relationship with his father was highly unsatisfactory because of the constraints and self-consciousness which characterized him and his son, that he was exposed to the corrupting influence of several unprincipled tutors and undermined by the double moral standard of the society in which he grew up. These facts, together with Adolphe's deep-seated desire for independence, explain in many ways the nature of his relationship with Ellénore and render its outcome inevitable. They ensure that the initial description of his character, and his subsequent actions and reactions, are of a piece. It is clear, however, that this coherence which the fictional character requires and receives is to some degree in conflict with his moral claim that he has no desire for self-justification. In fact, ostensibly artistic considerations convey the impression of an "arranged" self-portrait which weakens our belief in Adolphe's claims to complete candor. As a result, an atmosphere of moral ambiguity pervades the novel. At times, explanation is allowed to merge into justification, psychological necessity replaces moral responsibility, and an uneasy balance is maintained by Adolphe between statements which amount to saying that he is unable to help his behavior and others containing a confession that he should not have acted as he did.

This moral ambiguity gives *Adolphe* a humane and genuinely problematical dimension lacking in *Cécile*. The novel is enriched by an understanding presentation of moral inconsistency side by side with the suggestion that certain human dilemmas are beyond the reach of clear ethical solutions. Adolphe finds it equally impossible to love Ellénore or to leave her. Perhaps he should have behaved differently, yet we are made to understand why he acted as he did. Constant wrote in his preface to the second edition: "[Adolphe's] position, and that of Ellénore, allowed of no solution, and this is exactly what I intended. I showed him suffering torment because his love for Ellénore was not strong enough; and yet, if he had loved her more, his torment would not have been less." [24] The dilemma thus posed within the novel, in terms of psychological and moral reaction, though fulfilling the requirements of a fictional situation, is very close to Constant's own experience, shorn of precise autobiographical detail, at the time of writing. It conveys the flavor, not the facts, of his dilemma *vis-à-vis* Mme de Staël. By following the demands of art more boldly than he could ever do again, he brought indirect moral self-disclosure, and a direct application of the novelist's imaginative gifts, into a powerful and memorable relationship.

Adolphe relies for its effect, of course, on the character of Ellénore as well as on that of Adolphe. It is true that he is the sole narrator, and that we see Ellénore mainly through his eyes; nevertheless, she is not a mere cipher as has sometimes been suggested.[25] Just as Adolphe possesses greater moral complexity than the narrator in *Cécile*, so Ellénore is a more fully dimensional figure than either Cécile or Mme de Malbée. Once again, Constant appears to have created a more convincing fictional character by moving further away from immediate autobiographical considerations. Ellénore does not depend on the close relationship with a single real-life person that characterizes Cécile and Mme de Malbée (who have direct links with Charlotte von Hardenberg and Mme de Staël respectively). In the case of Ellénore, Constant goes beyond stylization and transforms autobiography into fiction by using four or five women whom he knew well in order to "compose" his heroine. He probably drew on Anna Lindsay, Julie Talma, Mme Trevor, Mme de Staël, and Charlotte, but the result is an imaginary character, coherent and independent, who is none of them. Paul Delbouille goes so far as to say that he cannot find a single fact or characteristic which can be associated more specifically with Charlotte, for example, than with Mme de Staël or Anna Lindsay.[26]

The composite figure of Ellénore, created in this way, is a fascinating one—particularly in the second chapter of the novel. Her qualities of devotion and pride are emphasized immediately, and we are also told that she could make no claim to intellectual distinction. What fascinates Adolphe first and foremost is what he calls "the bizarre nature of her situation." He gives a brilliant summary of her position as a kept woman, comte de P's mistress:

She possessed many prejudices, but all her prejudices ran counter to her own advantage. She set great store by regularity of conduct precisely because her own life was irregular by conventional standards. She was extremely religious because religion severely condemned her mode of existence. In conversation she sternly discouraged what other women would have regarded as harmless jokes because she continually feared that people would think themselves justified by her situation in making improper ones. She would have liked to receive in her home men of the highest rank only, and of irreproachable reputation, because those women with whom she shuddered to be compared normally move in rather mixed company and, becoming resigned to the loss of general respect, seek only friends who will amuse them. In a word, Ellénore was constantly at odds with her destiny.[27]

The description continues along these lines, with warnings of dangers to come in the comparison of Ellénore to a "beautiful tempest" and the statement that she was emotionally unstable because of the conflict between her deepest feelings and her social position. Indeed, the first two chapters of the novel contain all the essential elements of the tragic situation which develops in the remaining eight.

VI *Tragic Inevitability in* Adolphe

The main body of the novel is notable for the ways in which an implacable logic presides over the relationship established between the carefully composed figures of Adolphe and Ellénore.

Logical inevitability as such is not necessarily tragic, but in *Adolphe* it is identified with features of temperament which remorselessly create suffering for both parties. In the end, Ellénore dies and Adolphe is left desolate and alone, lamenting the very freedom which he thought was essential to him. In this sense, the novel is a tragedy of character rooted in the strengths and weaknesses of the two protagonists.

It is central to Adolphe's tragedy that his rationalism creates situations which his sensibility cannot accept. His father had protected him, as a youth, from the consequences of his actions, but there is no way in which his conscience can be anesthetized when confronted by the outcome for Ellénore of his *liaison* with her. To this extent his tragic status is intensified—and dignified—by the fact that some of his best qualities (e.g., his sense of loyalty, his sense of responsibility, and his feeling for the suffering of others) play a major part in provoking his dilemma. In Ellénore, too, we see admirable qualities leading to tragic consequences under the pressure of events. Her devotion and pride, confronted by Adolphe's inability to love rather than pity her, are gradually and inexorably transformed into a demanding possessiveness and tormenting despair which create further barriers between them.

This, then, is very much a tragedy of *two* people caught up in a web of relationships from which they cannot free themselves and in which they can only suffer. Constant's own view that two people suffer, though in different ways, when a man seduces a woman is clear from his preface to the second edition. He quickly outlines the familiar tragedy of the woman who mistook lust for love, who finds herself rejected, and whose trust in another human being leads to moral blame and social ostracism. Writing at more length about the man, he begins by suggesting, as a general rule, that most men are fundamentally less corrupt or fickle than they believe. The theoretical prospect of inflicting suffering may not greatly worry the potential seducer, but once faced by a woman who suffers because of the love he has inspired in her but denied to her, he cannot remain indifferent. At this point, he is bound to be morally diminished, and therefore to be damaged as a human being, whether he denies his own better nature and callously rejects the woman in question or, like Adolphe, allows his finer feelings to operate, can neither love nor leave the woman, and probably thereby inflicts even greater suffering on her.[28]

So far we have interpreted *Adolphe* only as a tragedy of character. Character, however, does not exist in a vacuum, least of all for Constant. Apart from an introductory "Note by the Publisher" and the ten chapters which follow, the novel contains two additional "documents." One is a letter, sent by an unnamed acquaintance of Adolphe and Ellénore, to the publisher who agrees to have their story printed. The other is a reply to this letter from the publisher himself. While the publisher takes the view that Adolphe was "punished for his character by his character" and that "circumstances amount to very little; character is everything," [29] the letter which he receives attributes Ellénore's tragedy to the influence of society and adds significantly: "Society is too powerful, expresses itself in too many ways, injects too much bitterness into a love affair which it has not sanctioned." [30] It has been suggested that Constant leaves the reader with the unresolved contradiction of these two judgments in order to suggest that to condemn another human being is at best an uncertain and hazardous undertaking.[31] But the second of the two judgments is also significant in the light of the numerous references made throughout the novel to the nature and role of society. Also, what Constant terms the characters' "destiny" is sometimes located in themselves, but also often placed in the social reality which surrounds them. In either case, it is not something transcendent in the sense, for example, of "providence." Rather, we are given to understand that people are what they are, and behave as they do, not least because of the way in which society first forms, and later judges, them.

As we have seen, Adolphe scorns the hypocrisy of a society which only condemns his *liaison* because of its public and persistent nature. But he also desires success within this society. He wants to rise through its hierarchies and obtain its fruits. Consequently, there is also a social dimension to his dilemma. Personal integrity or social advancement are the choices before him, but both are damaging. If he persists in repudiating the conventions of a society for which he feels contempt, all social outlets will be closed to his very real talents. If he buys social approval by sacrificing Ellénore, all self-respect will be lost. In either case, he will be damaged as a person. This is one of several ways in which the novel suggests that Constant (as we saw in Chapter 6) was particularly interested in that form of tragedy which involves some sort of conflict between the individual and the community.

VII *Formal Concentration in* Adolphe

In *Adolphe* Constant succeeds in handling a complex human drama with economy and clarity, yet without losing analytical depth. The novel is a mere hundred pages long in most editions, but a concise handling of words and a straightforward linear narrative leave room for a detailed exploration of the emotional impasse in which Adolphe and Ellénore become fatally enmeshed. Subplots, local color, an elaborate decor or a multiplicity of characters are all avoided. One is reminded of the spare concentration of Racinian tragedy as Constant begins with a short, clear, expository summary and then allows the two protagonists to act out their inevitable drama.

The fact that the story is told entirely by Adolphe himself makes formal concentration acceptable and natural. First-person narrative necessarily involves a certain restriction of viewpoint and this encourages sharpness of focus. The narrator is a man obsessed by a particular experience from his past. The fact that it absorbs his whole attention and allows of no distraction is reinforced by the firm and compact treatment of the narrative line. Indeed, one may claim that Constant's narrative style is an essential part of Adolphe's character as this latter progressively reveals itself through the story. At the same time, the narrative focus, though concentrated, is not a single one. Adolphe the narrator tells us about Adolphe the actor in the drama. While we are never in any doubt that they are the same person, and while we are thus enabled to relive Adolphe's past from the inside as it were, the two Adolphes are not identical. It is the narrator, not the young man contemplating the seduction of Ellénore, who wrote "I have no desire here to justify myself," and who comments toward the end of the novel, "I am writing this now with a feeling of remorse." [32] This double "I" is an inevitable part, of course, of any first-person narrative relating to the past. It has the particular advantage here, however, that it enables Constant to use the later knowledge which the older Adolphe possesses in order to introduce, in an unobtrusive way, a further sense of inevitability, even doom, with such phrases as "a first blow had been struck." [33]

Another kind of concentration is seen most clearly in the somewhat strange opening paragraph of Chapter 4. In contrast to the penetrating intellectual tone of much of the book, this is an ecstatic invocation of the "magic of love" which may at first suggest that the narrator has, after all, been temporarily distracted from his purpose. In fact, however, the passage fulfills an important function within the structure of the work. A hint concerning the nature of this function is contained in the contrast between the conventional rhetorical question at the beginning— "Magic of love, who can portray it!"—and the ironical final phrase—"Magic of love, which cannot be described by anyone who has experienced it!" Between these two phrases there is a carefully contrived description of the characteristics of love: its sweetness, tenderness, bliss, sense of security, etc. But in the light of the final comment, this description should be interpreted as a piece of self-deception on Adolphe's part. Indeed, his intimate relationship with Ellénore, which occupies the rest of the novel, gives the lie to all the qualities and experiences which he has attributed to love.

This outburst, though untypical of the Adolphe who narrates, is consistent with the younger Adolphe whose idealism and better nature made it impossible for him to desert Ellénore completely. By means of one short paragraph, therefore, and without doing violence to psychological consistency, Constant manages to place the remainder of the novel in an ironical perspective. The device is economical and effective. It enables Adolphe to convey irony unconsciously. There is no need for obtrusive intervention and comment by the author as author. This is typical of Constant's skill in *Adolphe*. Despite certain analytical remarks and universalizing maxims made by the hero, the main moral statements of the book are allowed to emerge from the characters' own reactions. They are not superimposed by the author in the form of discursive comment.

The types of economy and concentration described above are reinforced at the surface level by a network of associations and cross-references. Martin Turnell has indicated several words and images—"tempest," "inner sanctuary," or brief references to landscape—which echo one another at different points in the text.[34] Obviously, the novel is also concentrated and unified in the complex narrating personality of Adolphe himself. In fact, it is a closely interlocking structure at both the psychological and stylistic levels. Nevertheless, this intense focus in no way detracts from its broad human relevance and wide appeal. It belongs preeminently to the French analytical tradition in fiction which examines individual experience in a way that establishes general human truth. We are readily convinced, indeed, that the experience of Adolphe and Ellénore is a paradigm of the tragic misunderstanding that lies in wait for all human relationships. For this reason, Constant's greatest literary work has rightly been termed "a modern morality." [35]

CHAPTER 8

Conclusion

ALTHOUGH it has not been possible to examine Constant's gifts as a diarist or letter writer, a number of extracts quoted earlier will give some idea of his achievement in these fields. A brief additional word should be said, however, about *Le Cahier rouge*. This is the name now given to an autobiography which he began, and abandoned, in 1811. It was first published as late as 1907. On the surface, it is the most amusing of Constant's writings—witty, humorous, and possessing the narrative speed and verve of a picaresque novel. He recounts a series of youthful escapades and if the precise details are not always authentic, the flavor they are given is an accurate reflection of one side of his personality. *Le Cahier rouge* is certainly autobiographical and uses the real names of Constant's friends and acquaintances. But it also receives a measure of stylization for literary purposes. It is closer in manner to *Cécile* than to *Adolphe*, but in tone it is distinctly less sombre than either.

Nevertheless, beneath the rapid characterization, the deft narrative manner and the ironic style, a serious note is heard on various occasions. It arises from the fact that Constant returns several times to his uncertainty and timidity as a young man. This, in itself, may well be regarded as a normal feature of adolescence, yet one senses that the loneliness which Constant portrays, and the inability to make satisfactory contact with other human beings, remained with him throughout his life. One of the ironies inherent in the biography of this master of irony is the fact that he appears to have felt ultimately alone and unfulfilled in the midst of political activity, social success, and literary renown. His feverish love affairs and compulsive gambling bear all the desperate marks of Pascalian *divertissement*.

No doubt there is much in Constant's thought that is limited in value and interest by the particular assumptions and circumstances of his own age. His economic liberalism, enlightened and progressive in his day, has only very limited application to twentieth-century conditions. His determined individualism and emphasis on personal freedom still represent important goals, but the collectivist aspects of modern technology and mass communications make their realization much more difficult than most of his arguments would suggest.

It is when his ideas remain problematical, rather than become prescriptive, that Constant speaks directly to our own age. At the religious and philosophical levels, for example, he explored the shifting frontier between reason and faith, between rational analysis and intuitive understanding. He sought to give theism a new form which would satisfy both intellect and sensibility. Furthermore, he understood that metaphysical problems arise because individuals are fundamentally alienated, confused, and alone. Temperamentally, they need the support of absolutes which their minds cannot readily accept. Their attempts to escape from themselves in other human beings rather than in pure thought are also doomed to failure. It is because he believed these things that Constant was more concerned to understand than to judge. Throughout the range of his writings he repeatedly tells us that men are complex and contradictory beings who remain a problem both to themselves and to others. The problem is one to be explained rather than deplored.

In these circumstances, writing became for Constant, among other things, a possible defense against the unending flux of experience. Words were an attempt to establish fixed points in a dissolving personal world. In this sense, the clarity and precision of his prose is a stylistic feature which also met a temperamental need. In his political writings he used this clarity in order to explore what he considered to be the folly and confusion of his contemporaries while also offering them precisely articulated solutions. In his lifelong work on religion he attempted to underpin stylistic clarity with indisputable scholarly fact and thus produce a more lasting intellectual structure which would escape the action of time and allow him to be remembered long after his death. In his fictional writing, less ambitiously but in the end more effectively, he employed the same features of style—clarity and precision—in order to expound dilemmas existing well beyond the range of purely intellectualized solutions. This represents his greatest claim to our continuing attention.

Notes and References

Chapter One

1. *Pléiade*, pp. 256–57: *. . . je ne suis pas tout à fait un être réel. Il y a en moi deux personnes, dont une, observatrice de l'autre . . .* (Quotations from the Pléiade edition of the *Oeuvres* hereafter noted as *P*. All translations are my own.)

2. *P*, pp. 430–31: *Je ne puis me passer de femmes; elles me font un bien réel, et leur privation dérange toutes mes facultés physiques et morales* (11 February 1805).

3. *P*, p. 566: *J'aimerais bien mieux l'étude et la solitude que toutes les femmes et tous les amours du monde* (5 December 1806).

4. *Je suis las de cette étrange manie qui me fait voir successivement les côtés opposés d'un objet . . .* (Letter of 4 April 1794 to Mme de Charrière quoted in G. Rudler, *La Jeunesse de Benjamin Constant* [Paris: Armand Colin, 1909], p. 443).

5. *"Pourquoi, je vous prie, m'accuser d'un caractère faible? C'est une accusation à laquelle tous les gens éclairés sont exposés, parce qu'ils voient les deux, ou pour mieux dire, les mille côtés des objets, et qu'il leur est impossible de se décider, de sorte qu'ils ont l'air de chanceler tantôt d'un côté, tantôt de l'autre* (Letter of 23 January 1804 to Mme de Nassau quoted in D. Melegari (ed), *Journal intime de Benjamin Constant et lettres à sa famille et à ses amis* [Paris: Ollendorf, 1895], p. 378).

6. *P*, p. 801: *J'ai défendu quarante ans le même principe, liberté en tout, en religion, en philosophie, en littérature, en industrie, en politique: et par liberté, j'entends le triomphe de l'individualité, tant sur l'autorité qui voudrait gouverner par le despotisme, que sur les masses qui réclament le droit d'asservir la minorité à la majorité. Le despotisme n'a aucun droit. La majorité a celui de contraindre la minorité à respecter l'ordre: mais tout ce qui ne trouble pas l'ordre, tout ce qui n'est qu'intérieur comme l'opinion; tout ce qui, dans la manifestation de l'opinion, ne nuit pas à autrui, soit en provoquant des violences matérielles, soit en s'opposant à une manifestation contraire; tout ce qui, en fait d'industrie, laisse l'industrie rivale s'exercer librement, est individuel, et ne saurait être légitimement soumis au pouvoir social.*

7. *P*, p. 1071: *Il y a au contraire une partie de l'existence humaine qui, de nécessité, reste individuelle et indépendante, et qui est de droit hors de toute compétence sociale.*

8. *P*, p. 1014: *des prétextes à tous les genres de tyrannie.*

9. *P*, pp. 1010–11: *Cette liberté se composait plutôt de la participation active au pouvoir collectif que de la jouissance paisible de l'indépendance individuelle; et même, pour assurer cette participation, il était nécessaire que les citoyens sacrifiassent en grande partie cette jouissance; mais ce sacrifice est absurde à demander, impossible à obtenir à l'époque à laquelle les peuples sont arrivés.*

10. *P*, pp. 1012–13: *Les anciens trouvaient plus de jouissances dans leur existence publique, et ils en trouvaient moins dans leur existence privée: en conséquence, lorsqu'ils sacrifiaient la liberté individuelle à la liberté politique, ils sacrifiaient moins pour obtenir plus. Presque toutes les jouissances des modernes sont dans leur existence privée: l'immense majorité, toujours exclue du pouvoir, n'attache nécessairement qu'un intérêt très passager à son existence publique. En imitant les anciens, les modernes sacrifieraient donc plus pour obtenir moins.*

11. *P*, p. 1013: *Les anciens avaient sur toutes choses une conviction entière; nous n'avons presque sur rien qu'une conviction molle et flottante, sur l'incomplet de laquelle nous cherchons en vain à nous étourdir.*

12. See *P*, p. 97.

13. *P*, p. 878: *Nous n'envisageons l'amour que comme une passion de la même nature que toutes les passions humaines, c'est-à-dire ayant pour effet d'égarer notre raison, ayant pour but de nous procurer des jouissances. Les Allemands voient dans l'amour quelque chose de religieux, de sacré, une émanation de la divinité même, un accomplissement de la destinée de l'homme sur cette terre, un lien mystérieux et tout-puissant entre deux âmes qui ne peuvent exister que l'une pour l'autre. Sous le premier point de vue, l'amour est commun à l'homme et aux animaux; sous le second, il est commun à l'homme et à Dieu.*

14. *Je suis détaché de tout, sans intérêt, sans liens moraux . . .* (Quoted in Rudler, *op. cit.*, p. 389).

15. *J'aime ma femme pour 1000 bonnes qualités qu'elle a, mais la grande langueur où je suis plongé l'a aliénée; quand j'ai un moment de confiance ou de chaleur, elle est froide ou insouciante, et pour éviter une explication au-dessus de mes forces, je me tais et je m'en vais* (*Ibid.*, p. 389).

16. *P*, p. 83: *". . . la métaphysique la plus ingénieuse ne justifie pas l'homme qui a déchiré le cœur qui l'aimait."*

17. *Retraçons-nous ce que sûrement chacun de nous a éprouvé lorsque, forcé par les circonstances, il avait formé une résolution qui pouvait causer autour de lui une grande douleur. Que de fois, après*

*s'être affermi dans ses projets par le raisonnement, par le calcul, par
le sentiment d'une nécessité vraie ou supposée il a senti ses forces
l'abandonner à l'aspect de celui qu'il aurait affligé, ou à la vue des
larmes que faisaient couler ses premières paroles! Que de liaisons dont
la durée tient à cette cause! Combien souvent l'égoïsme ou la prudence
qui, solitaires, se croient invincibles, fléchissent devant la présence*
(Quoted in G. Poulet, *Benjamin Constant par lui-même* [Paris: Seuil,
1968], p. 86).

18. *Je suis convaincu que la véritable moralité est d'épargner le
plus qu'on peut de la douleur, et que c'est un devoir de sacrifier à ce
but, non seulement son propre bonheur, mais même, jusqu'à un certain
degré, les apparences et l'opinion* (J.-H. Menos [ed], *Lettres de Benjamin Constant à sa famille, 1775–1830* [Paris: Savine, 1888], p. 250).

19. *Chaque jour se ressemble, chaque heure est aujourd'hui ce que
la même heure était hier; et le temps s'enfuit, sans qu'excepté par mon
ouvrage qui avance, je puisse mettre une marque à aucun moment pour
le distinguer de ceux qui l'ont précédé ou de ceux qui vont le suivre*
(Letter of 23 September 1812 to Prosper de Barante, quoted in "Lettres à Prosper de Barante," *Revue des Deux Mondes,* vol. 34 (15 July
and 1 August 1906), 562).

20. . . . *l'homme ne se met pas une fois pour toutes en tête qu'il ne
vaut pas la peine de se tourmenter aujourd'hui quand on doit crever
demain. Thompson, l'auteur des Saisons, passait souvent des jours en-
tiers dans son lit; et quand on lui demandait pourquoi il ne se levait
pas:* 'I see no motive to rise, man,' *répondait-il. Ni moi non plus, je ne
vois de motif pour rien dans ce monde, et je n'ai de goût pour rien*
(Letter of 24 October 1790 to Mme de Charrière, quoted in Rudler,
op. cit., p. 383).

21. *Peut-être ai-je le malheur de sentir trop* . . . *que toutes nos
poursuites, tous nos efforts, tout ce que nous tentons, faisons, chan-
geons, ne sont que des jeux de quelques moments et ne peuvent mener
qu'à un anéantissement très prochain, que par conséquent nous n'avons
pas plus de motif pour acquérir de la gloire, pour conquérir un empire
ou pour faire un bon livre que nous n'en avons pour faire une pro-
menade ou une partie de whist, que le temps indépendent de nous va
d'un pas égal et nous entraîne également, soit que nous dormions ou
veillions, agissions ou nous tenions dans une inaction totale. Cette
vérité triviale et toujours oubliée est toujours présente à mon esprit, et
me rend presque insensible à tout* (Letter of 21 May [?] 1791 to Mme
de Charrière, quoted in Rudler, *op. cit.,* p. 386).

22. P, pp. 1391–9: *L'homme s'applaudit d'avoir repoussé tous les
préjugés, toutes les erreurs, toutes les craintes, et toutes les craintes,
tous les préjugés, toutes les erreurs semblent déchaînées. On a pro-
clamé l'empire de la raison, et tout l'univers est frappé de délire; tous*

les systèmes se fondent sur le calcul, s'adressent à l'intérêt, permettent le plaisir, recommandent le repos, et jamais les égarements ne furent plus honteux, les agitations plus désordonnées, les douleurs plus poignantes: c'est que dans ses attaques contre la forme qu'il a réduite en poussière, le scepticisme a porté atteinte au sentiment dont l'espèce humaine ne saurait se passer. L'homme, sorti vainqueur des combats qu'il a livrés, jette un regard sur le monde dépeuplé de puissances protectrices et demeure étonné de sa victoire. L'agitation de la lutte, l'idée du danger qu'il aimait à braver, la soif de reconquérir des droits contestés, toutes ces causes d'exaltation ne le soutiennent plus. Son imagination, naguère tout occupée d'un succès qu'on lui disputait encore, maintenant désœuvrée et comme déserte, se retourne sur elle-même. Il se trouve seul sur une terre qui doit l'engloutir. Sur cette terre, les générations se suivent, passagères, fortuites, isolées; elles paraissent, elles souffrent, elles meurent; nul lien n'existe entre elles. Aucune voix ne se prolonge des races qui ne sont plus aux races vivantes, et la voix des races vivantes doit s'abîmer bientôt dans le même silence éternel. Que fera l'homme sans souvenir, sans espoir, entre le passé qui l'abandonne et l'avenir fermé devant lui? Ses invocations ne sont plus écoutées, ses prières restent sans réponse. Il a repoussé tous les appuis dont ses prédécesseurs l'avaient entouré, il s'est réduit à ses propres forces. C'est avec elles qu'il doit affronter la satiété, la vieillesse, le remords, la foule innombrable des maux qui l'assiègent. Dans cet état violent et contre nature, ses actions sont un démenti perpétuel de ses raisonnements, ses terreurs une constante expiation de ses railleries. On le dirait frappé d'un double vertige, tantôt insultant à ce qu'il révère, tantôt tremblant devant ce qu'il vient de fouler aux pieds.

Chapter Two

1. *Je n'ai jamais compris ce qu'il faisait à Brunswick, encore moins ce que c'est que d'être gentilhomme de la chambre d'un duc despote, lorsqu'on est né républicain et qu'on en a les sentiments et les opinions* (Entry of 11 May 1794 in Charles de Constant's *Journal* quoted by Rudler, *op. cit.*, p. 440).

2. Members of the *sections* or local constituency divisions of Paris under the Commune. There were forty-eight *sections* which proved convenient centers of revolutionary activity.

3. *Je m'occupe à présent à lire et à réfuter le livre de Burke contre les* levellers *français. Il y a autant d'absurdités que de lignes dans ce fameux livre; aussi a-t-il un plein succès dans toutes les sociétés anglaises et allemandes. Il défend la noblesse, et l'exclusion des sectaires, et l'établissement d'une religion dominante, et autres choses de cette nature. . . . Je crois comme vous qu'on ne voit au fond que la fourbe et la fureur; mais j'aime mieux la fourbe et la fureur qui renversent les*

Notes and References

châteaux forts, détruisent les titres et autres sottises de cette espèce, mettent sur un pied égal toutes les rêveries religieuses, que celles qui voudraient conserver et consacrer ces misérables avortons de la stupidité barbare des Juifs, entée sur la férocité ignorante des Vandales. Le genre humain est né sot et mené par des fripons, c'est la règle; mais entre fripons et fripons, je donne ma voix aux Mirabeau et aux Barnave plutôt qu'aux Sartine et aux Breteuil (Letter of 10 December 1790 to Mme de Charrière quoted by Rudler, *op. cit.*, pp. 474–75). The final phrase here expresses Constant's preference for opponents of despotism over politicians who were closely identified with the monarchy.

4. *Si alors de nouveaux Marat, Robespierre, etc., viennent la troubler et qu'ils ne soient pas aussitôt écrasés qu'apparus, j'abandonne l'humanité, et j'abjure le nom d'homme* (Letter of 12 October 1793 to Mme de Charrière quoted by Rudler, *op. cit.*, p. 480).

5. *Qui veut le but veut les moyens, et je me lasse de mon inconséquence* (Letter of 6 and 7 June to Mme de Charrière quoted by Rudler, *op. cit.*, p. 486).

6. This means the ninth day of the month Thermidor, i.e., 27 July. The so-called Republican Calendar, which first became law on 5 October 1793, lasted for twelve years. It ran, retrospectively, from 22 September 1792—the day on which the Republic was proclaimed. The year thus began with the autumnal equinox and the months were renamed by the poet Fabre d'Églantine in a way that suggested their seasonal characteristics: Vendémiaire (22 September–21 October), Brumaire, Frimaire, Nivôse, Pluviôse, Ventôse, Germinal, Floréal, Prairial, Messidor, Thermidor, Fructidor. A major motive behind this new arrangement was a desire to destroy the Church calendar and abolish the Christian year.

7. Crane Brinton, *A Decade of Revolution, 1789–1799* (New York: Harper Torchbooks, 1963), pp. 194–95.

8. These three letters are published in full in Béatrice W. Jasinski, *L'Engagement de Benjamin Constant: Amour et Politique (1794–1796)* (Paris: Minard, 1971), pp. 110–25.

9. *Mon ami, vous vous trompez. C'est précisément en se présentant ainsi comme des accusés qui craignent un jugement, et qui, pour le rendre impossible, occupent la place des juges; c'est en conservant ainsi son pouvoir, non comme un moyen de bien public, mais comme une égide, que la Convention sa perdrait* (see Jasinski, *op. cit.*, p. 117).

10. *C'est donc au nom de votre intérêt, comme au nom de la république; au nom des membres qui seraient conservés dans l'assemblée, comme au nom de ceux qui en seraient exclus, que je vous adjure de renoncer à une idée qui, sous le prétexte frivole d'une sûreté précaire et illusoire, serait un aveu terrible de vos craintes et de vos remords, et qui, par l'improbation universelle qu'elle ne pourrait manquer d'in-*

spirer, créerait le danger même auquel vous vous flattez d'échapper (see Jasinski, *op. cit.*, p. 124).

11. See J.-J. Coulmann, *Réminiscences* (Paris: Lévy, 1862–69), 3 vols., Vol. III, pp. 54–55.

12. *Ibid.*

13. This letter is printed in full in Jasinski, *op. cit.*, pp. 134–41.

14. Constant was particularly opposed to the decision by the Directory to obtain a large, forced loan from the more affluent citizens.

15. *C'est en louant les hommes qu'on les pousse vers le bien; c'est en se montrant persuadé qu'ils ne peuvent se refuser aux actions honnêtes, qu'on les force à ces actions.*

16. *Hommes de tous les systèmes! . . . ralliez vous à un gouvernement, qui vous offre la paix et la liberté, et qui ne peut s'écrouler, qu'en vous ensevelissant sous ses ruines.*

17. *Les actes en petit nombre, qu'on reproche aux premiers moments d'une République qui a besoin de s'établir.*

18. *. . . au sortir du nuage impénétrable, qui couvre sa naissance, nous voyons le genre humain s'avancer vers l'égalité, sur les débris d'institutions de tout genre.*

19. *. . . cette inactivité est la source d'un de nos plus grands malheurs, d'un malheur qui n'est pas seulement politique, mais individuel, de ce sentiment aride et dévorant, qui consume notre existence, qui décolore tous les objets, et qui, semblable aux vents brûlants de l'Afrique, dessèche et flétrit tout ce qu'il rencontre. Ce sentiment, que ne peuvent désigner ni les langues anciennes, ni celle du seul peuple qui fut libre, dans l'Europe moderne, avant les Français, naît principalement de cette privation de but, d'intérêts et d'espérances autres qu'étroites et personnelles. Il poursuit, non seulement l'obscur sujet des Monarchies, mais les Rois sur leurs trônes, et les ministres dans leurs palais, parce que l'âme est toujours resserrée, lorsqu'elle est repoussée dans l'egoïsme.*

20. Text reprinted in O. Pozzo di Borgo (ed), *Écrits et discours politiques par Benjamin Constant* (Paris: Pauvert, 1964), Vol. 1, pp. 21–91.

21. *. . . le grand ennemi de toute liberté, le vice corrupteur de toute institution, le germe de mort qu'on ne peut ni modifier, ni mitiger, mais qu'il faut détruire.*

22. *Une constitution est la garantie de la liberté d'un peuple: par conséquent, tout ce qui tient à la liberté est constitutionnel, et, par conséquent aussi, rien n'est constitutionnel de ce qui n'y tient pas.*

23. Text reprinted in O. Pozzo di Borgo, *op. cit.*, Vol. 1, pp. 93–112.

24. Text reprinted in O. Pozzo di Borgo, *op. cit.*, Vol. 1, pp. 115–28.

25. Text reprinted in O. Pozzo di Borgo, *op. cit.*, Vol. 1, pp. 139–53.

26. Text reprinted in O. Pozzo di Borgo, *op. cit.*, Vol. 1, pp. 156–89.

27. *Il est facile de dire que ceux qui repoussent ce projet de loi plaident la cause des brigands, mettent obstacle au rétablissement de l'ordre et de la sûreté publique, entravent l'action nécessaire d'une justice rapide contre les ennemis de l'état social.*

Aussi, mes collègues, je ne serais pas monté à cette tribune, si je ne m'étais fait une règle de ne me laisser influencer jamais par des considérations de cette nature: lorsqu'on y cède une fois, il est impossible de prévoir jusqu'où elles conduisent, et jusqu'à quel degré déplorable la crainte d'interprétations peu méritées fait fléchir notre conscience, et nous fait dévier de nos devoirs.

Chapter Three

1. E. Legouis and L. Cazamian, *A History of English Literature* (London: Dent, 1945), pp. 973–74.

2. *Il existe . . . des principes politiques, indépendants de toute constitution et ces principes me semblent encore utiles à développer. Applicables à tous les gouvernements . . . compatibles avec la royauté comme avec la république, quelles que soient les formes de l'une et de l'autre, ces principes peuvent être discutés avec franchise et confiance* (quoted in O. Pozzo di Borgo, *op. cit.*, Vol. 1, 240).

3. *Rien fait. J'ai au fond du cœur une douleur amère de ma vie si mal arrangée. Le moment décisif est venu. Carrière occupée et honorable ou repos complet, ou mort. Cet été en décidera. . . .* (P, p. 672).

4. A dozen letters, mostly by Constant, are published in Bengt Hasselrot (ed), *Benjamin Constant: Lettres à Bernadotte* (Geneva: Droz, Lille: Giard, 1952). There is also an excellent introduction.

5. Printed in Hasselrot, *op. cit.*, pp. 3–6.

6. See *P*, p. 192.

7. *La guerre est donc antérieure au commerce. L'une est l'impulsion sauvage, l'autre le calcul civilisé* (P, p. 959).

8. *La variété, c'est de l'organisation; l'uniformité, c'est du mécanisme. La variété, c'est la vie; l'uniformité, c'est la mort* (P, p. 984).

9. *Sur tout le reste, le grand mot aujourd'hui, c'est l'uniformité. C'est dommage qu'on ne puisse abattre toutes les villes pour les rebâtir toutes sur le même plan, niveler toutes les montagnes, pour que le terrain soit partout égal: et je m'étonne qu'on n'ait pas ordonné à tous les habitants de porter le même costume, afin que le maître ne rencontrât plus de bigarrure irrégulière et de choquante variété* (P, p. 980).

10. Quoted in Harold Nicolson, *Benjamin Constant* (London: Constable, 1949), p. 214.

11. See *P*, pp. 997–98.
12. See *P*, pp. 1587–89.
13. Reprinted in Hasselrot, *op. cit.*, pp. 33–4.
14. *Napoléon ne s'est pas engagé à la clémence.* . . . *C'est Attila, c'est Gengis-Khan, plus terrible et plus odieux parce que les ressources de la civilisation sont à son usage. J'ai voulu la liberté sous diverses formes; j'ai vu qu'elle était possible sous la monarchie; j'ai vu le roi se rallier à la nation. Je n'irai pas, misérable transfuge, me traîner d'un pouvoir à l'autre, couvrir l'infamie par le sophisme et balbutier des mots profanés pour racheter une vie honteuse* (quoted in P. Bastid, *Benjamin Constant et sa doctrine* (Paris: A. Colin, 1966), Vol. 1, p. 280).
15. *On m'a reproché, dans une libelle, de ne m'être pas fait tuer auprès du trône que, le 19 mars, j'avais défendu; c'est que, le 20, j'ai levé les yeux, j'ai vu que le trône avait disparu, et que la France restait encore* (Constant, *Mémoires sur les Cent Jours*, Paris: Pichon et Didier, 1829, (1st ed. 1820–22), Pt, 1, p. 117).
16. See Nicolson, *op. cit.*, pp. 228–29.
17. *Nous voyons la pairie héréditaire dans la Grande-Bretagne, compatible avec un haut degré de liberté civile et politique: tous les citoyens qui se distinguent peuvent y parvenir. Elle n'a pas le seul caractère odieux de l'hérédité, le caractère exclusif. Le lendemain de la nomination d'un simple citoyen à la pairie, il jouit des mêmes privilèges légaux que le plus ancien des pairs* (*P*, p. 1097).
18. *Si nous voulons jouir une fois complètement en France des bienfaits du gouvernement représentatif, il faut adopter l'élection directe. C'est elle qui depuis 1788 porte dans la chambre des communes britannique tous les hommes éclairés. L'on aurait peine à citer un Anglais distingué par ses talents politiques, que l'élection n'ait pas honoré, s'il l'a briguée* (*P*, p. 1099).
19. See *P*, p. 1598.
20. *L'abolition de la propriété serait destructive de la division du travail, base du perfectionnement de tous les arts et de toutes les sciences. La faculté progressive, espoir favori des écrivains que je combats, périrait faute de temps et d'indépendance, et l'égalité grossière et forcée qu'ils nous recommandent, mettrait un obstacle invincible à l'établissement graduel de l'égalité véritable, celle du bonheur et des lumières* (*P*, p. 1168).
21. See W.W. Holdheim, *Benjamin Constant* (London: Bowes & Bowes, 1961), p. 80.
22. Timon [L.-M. Cormenin], *Le Livre des orateurs* (Paris: Pagnerre, 1842), pp. 336 and 341.
23. See *P*, pp. 1287–95 and pp. 1303–7.

Notes and References

Chapter Four

1. *Toutes les fois que l'on croit remarquer qu'il y a eu abus de lumières, c'est qu'il y avait manque de lumières. Toutes les fois qu'on accuse la vérité d'avoir fait du mal, ce mal n'a pas été l'effet de la vérité, mais de l'erreur. Dire que la vérité peut être dangereuse, c'est proférer une terrible accusation contre la Providence, qui a mis au rang des besoins de l'homme la recherche de la vérité* (Quoted in O. Pozzo di Borgo, *op. cit.*, Vol. 1, 201).

2. *Si un citoyen est arrêté arbitrairement, qu'importe à ce citoyen et à ses proches qu'un projet de loi, qui supprime ses plaintes, favorise les bons auteurs?* (*P*, p. 1253).

3. *Les gouvernements qui paraissent ne gêner en rien l'éducation particulière, favorisent néanmoins toujours les établissements qu'ils ont fondés, en exigeant de tous les candidats aux places relatives à l'éducation publique une sorte d'apprentissage dans ces établissements. Ainsi, le talent qui a suivi la route indépendante, et qui, par un travail solitaire, a réuni peut-être plus de connaissances, et probablement plus d'originalité qu'il ne l'aurait fait dans la routine des classes, trouve sa carrière naturelle, celle dans laquelle il peut se communiquer et se reproduire, fermée tout-à-coup devant lui* (*Commentaire sur l'ouvrage de Filangieri*, Part Four, Ch. 1).

4. *Messieurs, au nom de l'humanité, dans cette cause où toutes les distinctions de parti doivent disparaître, unissez-vous à moi pour réclamer la loi que le ministère nous avait promise. Exigeons, sous peine de refuser les fonds demandés, que dans cette session même la loi soit présentée. La session sera de quelques jours plus longue; mais des milliers de créatures humaines échapperont au sort dont un plus long retard les menace, et nous n'aurons pas accumulé sur nos têtes la responsibilité de toutes les atrocités qui se commettent au moment où je vous parle à cette tribune; que, dans cette loi surtout, soit réprimé un abus, dont le ministre est convenu l'année dernière, et qu'il a paru regarder comme une chose toute naturelle. Lorsque les Anglais prennent et confisquent les vaisseaux négriers, ils émancipent les nègres. Quand on a demandé à M. le ministre ce qu'on faisait des nègres confisqués au Sénégal, il a répondu qu'ils devenaient la propriété du gouvernement, et se livraient aux travaux de la colonie. A travers cette expression si douce, Messieurs, une vérité perce, c'est que malgré les promesses, les traités, les ordonnances royales, la traite se fait au profit du gouvernement* (*P*, pp. 1294–95).

5. See *Commentaire sur l'ouvrage de Filangieri*, Part Two, Ch. 2.

6. *Cette portion du public, qui rougirait d'assassiner et de voler sur la grande route, prend part sans scrupule à un commerce qui la séduit par ses bénéfices; et elle s'étourdit par des sophismes pour se déguiser*

*qu'entre elle et le meurtrier ou l'incendiaire il y a au moins parité.
Quand cette vérité sera bien reconnue; quand les lois ne mettront point
de différence entre des crimes au moins égaux; quand, indépendamment
des lois, l'opinion indignée poursuivra dans les rues et sur les places
publiques le négociant qui aura pris part à la traite, la presque totalité
de la population commerçante refusera d'y tremper . . .*
    *C'est donc à produire cette conviction morale qu'il faut travailler
sans relâche. Il ne faut plus simplement, comme Filangieri, se borner
à poser des principes, à prouver qu'en théorie la traite est une violation
de tous les droits; il faut démontrer par des faits qu'elle est en pratique
l'accumulation de tous les crimes. Il faut reproduire tous les traits de
cruauté dont elle souille encore aujourd'hui les annales maritimes de
toutes les nations (Ibid.).*
    7. *. . . Qu'ils apprennent au moins quelle est la religion qu'ils com-
battent avant que de la combattre (Pensées: 427 [Lafuma], 194
[Brunschvicg]).*
    8. *P, p. 1184.*
    9. *. . . la puissance du sacrifice, qui est la source de toute vertu
(P, p. 1185).*
    10. *. . . cette partie vague et profonde de nos sensations morales, qui
par sa nature même défie tous les efforts du langage (P, p. 1186).*
    11. *Comment définirez-vous l'impression d'une nuit obscure, d'une
antique forêt, du vent qui gémit à travers des ruines, ou sur des tom-
beaux, de l'océan qui se prolonge au-delà des regards? Comment définirez-vous l'émotion que vous causent les chants d'Ossian, l'église de
Saint-Pierre, la méditation de la mort, l'harmonie des sons ou celle des
formes? Comment définirez-vous la rêverie, ce frémissement intérieur
de l'âme où viennent se rassembler et comme se perdre, dans une confusion mystérieuse, toutes les puissances des sens et de la pensée? Il y
a de la religion au fond de toutes ces choses. Tout ce qui est beau,
tout ce qui est intime, tout ce qui est noble, participe à la religion
(P, p. 1186).*
    12. *L'intolérance, en plaçant la force du côté de la foi, a placé le
courage du côté du doute (P, p. 1187).* Most of these ideas, often in
an identical formulation, occur in the first chapter of *De la religion,*
Vol. 1.
    13. *Quand la religion dégénère de la sorte, elle perd toute son in-
fluence sur la morale; elle se loge, pour ainsi dire, dans une case des
têtes humaines, où elle reste isolée de tout le reste de l'existence. Nous
voyons en Italie la messe précéder le meurtre, la confession le suivre,
la pénitence l'absoudre, et l'homme ainsi délivré du remords, se pré-
parer à des meurtres nouveaux (P, p. 1193).*
    14. *Il en est de la religion comme des grandes routes: j'aime que*

l'État les entretienne, pourvu qu'il laisse à chacun le droit de préférer les sentiers (P, p. 1197).

15. *La douleur réveille en nous, tantôt ce qu'il y a de plus noble dans notre nature, le courage, tantôt ce qu'il y a de plus tendre, la sympathie et la pitié. Elle nous apprend à lutter pour nous, à sentir pour les autres (De la religion, Vol. 4, p. 268).*

Chapter Five

1. Pierre Deguise, *Benjamin Constant méconnu: Le Livre de la Religion avec des documents inédits* (Genève: Droz, 1966). Helen H. S. Hogue, *On Changes in Benjamin Constant's Books on Religions* (Genève: Droz, 1964). Patrice Thompson, *Deux Chapitres inédits de l'Esprit des Religions (1803–1804)* (Genève: Droz, 1970). Henri Gouhier, *Benjamin Constant* (Paris: Desclée de Brouwer ["Les Écrivains devant Dieu"], 1967).

2. See Gouhier, *op. cit.*, pp. 18–20.

3. Joseph de Maistre, *Considérations sur la France* (1797), quoted by Gouhier, *op. cit.*, p. 19.

4. *Nourri des principes de la philosophie du XVIII⁰ siècle et surtout des ouvrages d'Helvétius, je n'avais d'autre pensée que de contribuer pour ma part à la destruction de ce que j'appelais les préjugés. Je m'étais emparé d'une assertion de l'auteur de l'Esprit, qui prétend que la religion païenne était de beaucoup préférable au christianisme; et je voulais appuyer cette assertion, que je n'avais ni approfondie, ni examinée, de quelques faits pris au hasard et de beaucoup d'épigrammes et de déclamations que je croyais neuves (P, p. 95).*

5. *Je sens plus que jamais le néant de tout, combien tout promet et rien ne tient, combien nos forces sont au-dessus de notre destination, et combien cette disproportion doit nous rendre malheureux. . . . Il prétend que Dieu, c'est-à-dire l'auteur de nous et de nos alentours, est mort avant d'avoir fini son ouvrage . . . que tout à présent se trouve fait dans un but qui n'existe plus, et que nous, en particulier, nous sentons destinés à quelque chose dont nous ne nous faisons aucune idée; nous sommes comme des montres où il n'y aurait point de cadran, et dont les rouages, doués d'intelligence, tourneraient jusqu'à ce qu'ils fussent usés, sans savoir pourquoi et se disant toujours: puisque je tourne, j'ai donc un but. Cette idée me paraît la folie la plus spirituelle et la plus profonde que j'aie ouïe, et bien préférable aux folies chrétiennes, musulmanes ou philosophiques, des 1er, 6ᵉ et 18ᵉ siècles de notre ère* (Letter of 4 June 1790 to Mme de Charrière, quoted in Rudler, *op. cit.*, pp. 376–77).

6. See Rudler, *op. cit.*, p. 385.

7. *Je ne voi (sic) aucune preuve, aucune probabilité qu'il y ait un Dieu, quoique je vous jure que je désirerais bien qu'il y en eût un.*

Cela changerait toute mon existence. . . . Je voi que la morale est vague, que l'homme est méchant, faible, sot et vil, et je crois qu'il n'est destiné qu'à être tel (Letter of 6 July 1792 to Mme de Charrière, quoted in Rudler, *op. cit.*, p. 390).

8. *La religion a cela d'admirable, c'est très sérieusement que je le dis, elle a cela d'admirable que les antécédents ne la gênent pas. On la greffe sur l'ambition, sur l'amour, sur toutes les passions et la greffe prend à tout âge* (Letter of 9 September 1807 to Mme de Nassau. See *Lettres de Benjamin Constant à sa famille, 1775–1830* [ed. Menos], p. 227).

9. See *P*, pp. 173–75. Constant refers to the sect as Pietists rather than Quietists. It is usual, however, to distinguish clearly between Pietism (which emphasized the need for personal salvation) and Quietism. The former is associated with German Protestantism and the latter with the Catholicism of Molinos, Fénelon, and Mme Guyon (see R. A. Knox, *Enthusiasm* [Oxford: Clarendon Press, 1950], p. 398 and *passim*).

10. *. . . cette étroite et cynique philosophie, qui, dans Voltaire, nous faisait naître entre l'urine et la matière fécale, dans Helvétius ne nous distinguait des chevaux que par les mains, dans Diderot voulait étrangler le dernier prêtre avec les boyaux du dernier roi, et dans Cabanis définissait la pensée comme une sécrétion du cerveau* ("Lettres de Benjamin Constant à Prosper de Barante, 1805–1830," *Revue des deux mondes*, Vol. XXXIV, [1906], 549).

11. *Ma religion consiste en deux points: vouloir ce que Dieu veut, c'est-à-dire lui faire l'hommage de notre cœur; ne rien nier, c'est-à-dire lui faire l'hommage de notre esprit* (*Revue des deux mondes, loc. cit.*, p. 269).

12. See Pierre Deguise, *op. cit.*, pp. 270–71.

13. *. . . mon ouvrage sera bien dans votre sens. J'y ai été conduit par une foule innombrable de faits, envisagés avec d'autant plus d'impartialité que je les ai recueillis dans un sens contraire, et que mes habitudes et la direction de mes idées m'ont même porté longtemps à leur faire une sorte de violence pour les plier à l'intention de mon entreprise. Mais comme j'étais de bonne foi, la violence n'y a rien fait. Les preuves ont réagi sur moi, le cœur humain s'est montré ce qu'il est quand le sentiment religieux en est banni, et le sentiment religieux lui-même n'a pu longtemps me satisfaire, impuissant et vague qu'il est, lorsqu'il est abandonné à ses propres forces. J'ai vu l'homme incrédule se précipitant dans la magie. J'ai vu l'homme fatigué de l'incrédulité et ne pouvant mettre à sa place que l'extase, un enthousiasme sans frein, et des exagérations d'autant plus incurables qu'elles partaient du raisonnement, et marchaient méthodiquement à la folie. J'ai vu la raison dans toute sa pompe et dans toute sa faiblesse, le résultat de quatre*

siècles de méditations n'être d'abord que le chaos, puis une ordonnance fantastique et arbitraire, l'homme parvenant à tout détruire et hors d'état de rien rétablir, et succombant enfin sous tant d'évidences irrésistibles, j'ai vu Dieu rendant à l'homme non seulement la religion, mais la raison même.

Depuis que je me suis franchement avoué ces vérités, je ne sais quelle simplicité merveilleuse s'est répandue sur mon ouvrage. Ma route si incertaine pendant tant d'années, s'est tout à coup présentée à moi, claire et unie. J'ai vu toutes mes idées se ranger dans un ordre que tous mes efforts n'avaient jusqu'alors pu découvrir. J'ai vu les grandes énigmes se résoudre.

La philosophie allemande me sert beaucoup, quoiqu'elle ne marche pas dans une direction parfaitement analogue à la mienne. Elle marche dans le sens dont je me suis écarté, mais qui suit pourtant une ligne parallèle. . . . C'est une philosophie un peu vague, mais respectant tout ce qui est religieux, retrouvant la religion dans tout ce qui est bon et s'agitant seulement dans ses tentatives pour généraliser ses idées, et placer la divinité dans tout, afin de parvenir à un résultat plus séduisant par son universalité apparente (Revue des deux mondes, loc. cit., pp. 548–49).

14. See *P*, p. 759.

15. See *P*, p. 764.

16. See *P*, p. 760.

17. *Vous m'avez dit que j'avais droit à des miracles de votre part. A Dieu ne plaise que j'en exige et que je tente la bonté céleste! Mais si vous pouvez en faire, des miracles, faites-en un pour me sauver. Le temps presse* (Letter published in *Journal de Genève* for 9 March 1908 and reprinted in Gouhier, *op. cit.*, pp. 121–23).

18. See J. Mistler (ed), *Benjamin Constant et Madame de Staël, Lettres à un ami. Cent onze lettres inédites à Claude Hochet . . .* (Neuchâtel: A la Baconnière, 1949), p. 194.

19. For details of these changes, and of the complicated collection of manuscripts, see Hogue, *op. cit.*, Thompson, *op. cit.*, and Bastid, *op. cit.*, Vol. 2, pp. 591–605.

20. See, for example, *De la religion*, Vol. 1, p. 180: *. . . ce sentiment religieux, quelque grossier qu'il paraisse encore, est plus noble et plus raisonnable que tous les systèmes qui ne voient dans la vie qu'un phénomène fortuit . . .*

21. In *Du polythéisme romain*, Vol. 1, Ch. 4, he specifically links Roman polytheism with agriculture.

22. *En tâchant de se figurer les dieux revêtus de toute la beauté, la majesté, la vertu qu'il peut concevoir, il s'exerce à réfléchir sur ces choses, et sa morale gagne à ses réflexions* (*De la religion*, Vol. 3, p. 402).

23. *L'absurdité de certaines formes religieuses, loin d'être un argument contre la religion, est une démonstration que nous ne pouvons nous en passer (De la religion,* Vol. 4, pp. 42–43).

24. *Ainsi, le polythéisme romain protégeait, de sa puissance invisible et mystérieuse, des institutions qui n'étaient pas sans doute parfaites, mais qui certes obtiendront notre respect, si nous réfléchissons qu'un grand peuple leur a dû six siècles de liberté (Du polythéisme romain,* Vol. 1, p. 53).

25. *. . . . violemment, mais avec maladresse par l'autorité, scandaleusement et sans conviction par les prétres, faiblement et avec indecision par les philosophes qui se dévouent à sa cause . . . (Du polythéisme romain,* Vol. 2, p. 294).

26. *Le théisme a enfin sur le Polythéisme cette incontestable supériorité, qu'il jette dans l'esprit de l'homme je ne sais quelle idée, ou plutôt quelle sensation de l'infini. Cette idée, cette sensation est plus favorable à la morale que toute doctrine fixe, dogmatique et positive. L'absence de bornes appliquée à nos sentimens et à nos pensées, est ce qui tend le plus à épurer les uns et à élever les autres. Toutes les passions généreuses reposent sur cette notion, même quand elle est inaperçue. L'amour n'est anobli, l'amour n'est épuré que parce qu'aussi longtemps qu'il dure, il croit ne devoir pas finir (Du polythéisme romain,* Vol. 2, p. 311).

27. *On voit disparaître le pouvoir oppressif des corporations, les principes injustes de l'intolérance, les notions étroites qui rabaissent la religion au rang d'un trafic, ou qui attachent à des pratiques minutieuses une importance exagérée, mais le fond survit à cette destruction des formes, et l'homme a de nouveau fait un pas immense vers l'anoblissement de sa nature et vers son éternelle destinée (Du polythéisme romain,* Vol. 2, p. 317).

Chapter Six

1. Quoted in L. Morel, "L'Influence germanique chez Mme de Charrière et chez Benjamin Constant," *Revue d'histoire littéraire de la France,* Vol. XIX (1912), 102.

2. *. . . les progrès de la littérature, quelque séparée qu'on aime à la concevoir de toute idée politique, tiennent toujours, non pas sans doute à une liberté explicite et garantie, mais à un mouvement dans les esprits qui n'est jamais complètement étranger aux souvenirs, à la possession, à l'espérance, au sentiment, en un mot, de la liberté (P,* p. 854).

3. For Constant's comments on Sophocles and Euripides see *P,* pp. 251, 253 and 259–60.

4. See *P,* p. 270.

5. *Difficulté de faire entrer la poésie allemande dans une tête ac-*

coutumée à la poésie française. La poésie française a toujours un but autre que la beauté poétique. C'est de la morale, ou de l'utilité, ou de l'expérience, ou de la finesse, ou du persiflage, enfin toujours de la réflexion. En conséquence, la poésie n'y existe jamais que comme véhicule ou comme moyen. Il n'y a pas ce vague, cet abandon à des sensations réfléchies, cette description tellement naturelle, tellement commandée par l'impulsion, que l'auteur ne paraît pas s'apercevoir qu'il décrit, enfin ce qui fait le caractère de la poésie allemande, et ce qui, depuis que je la connais, me paraît être le caractère essentiel de la véritable poésie. Le Français et l'Anglais vous disent: "Voyez comme je décris les objets." L'Allemand: "Voici comme les objets me frappent". . . . *Mais il résulte de là que les gens accoutumés à chercher dans la poésie autre chose que la poésie ne trouvent pas dans la poésie allemande ce qu'ils cherchent, et comme un mathématicien disait d'*Iphigénie *"Qu-est-ce que cela prouve?" les étrangers disent de la poésie allemande: "Où cela mène-t-il?"* (P, pp. 272–73).

6. *Au reste, Chateaubriand a mis si peu de raison, ou plutôt tant de folie, dans le reste de ses cinq volumes, qu'il n'est pas étonnant qu'ayant voulu être raisonnable une fois, il ait trouvé une quantité de bon sens disponible* (Letter of 6 November 1805 to the Comtesse de Nassau quoted in D. Melegari, *Journal intime de Benjamin Constant et lettres à sa famille et à ses amis* (Paris: Albin Michel, 1928), pp. 401–02).

7. See *P*, p. 831.

8. *Un ouvrage d'imagination ne doit pas avoir un but moral, mais un résultat moral. Il doit ressembler, à cet égard, à la vie humaine qui n'a pas un but, mais qui toujours a un résultat dans lequel la morale trouve nécessairement sa place* (P, p. 834).

9. E.g., see *Journal* for 13 November 1807.

10. *En ne peignant qu'une passion au lieu d'embrasser tout un caractère individuel, on obtient des effets plus constamment tragiques, parce que les caractères individuels, toujours mélangés, nuisent à l'unité de l'impression. Mais la vérité y perd peut-être encore.* . . . *D'ailleurs il y a bien moins de variété dans les passions propres à la tragédie que dans les caractères individuels, tels que les crée la nature. Les caractères sont innombrables; les passions théâtrales sont en petit nombre* (P, p. 869).

11. See *P*, pp. 865–67.

12. See Chapter 1 above, p.

13. See *P*, p. 883.

14. *Quand nous allons au théâtre, nous voulons voir mieux que nos amis* (P, p. 908).

15. . . . *ou de supprimer des caractères tout ce qui ne sert pas à l'action, et à plus forte raison, tout ce qui la contrarie . . . ou de con-*

server des traits individuels, au risque de rompre l'unité et de désorienter l'auditeur (P, p. 910).
16. See *P,* p. 910.

Chapter Seven

1. *P,* p. 558.
2. Major discussions of the genesis of *Cécile* and *Adolphe* will be found in: P. Bénichou, "La Genèse d'*Adolphe*," *Revue d'histoire littéraire de la France,* 54 (1954), 332–56; J.-H. Bornecque (ed), *Adolphe* (Paris: Garnier, 1963); P. Deguise, "*Adolphe* et les *Journaux intimes* de Benjamin Constant," *Revue des sciences humaines,* 82 (1956), 125–51; A. Oliver, "*Cécile* et la genèse d'*Adolphe*," *Revue des sciences humaines,* 93 (1967), 5–28; A. R. Pugh, "*Adolphe* et *Cécile*," *Revue d'histoire littéraire de la France,* 63 (1963), 415–23; P. Reboul's review article on Bornecque's edition of *Adolphe* in *Revue des sciences humaines,* 82 (1956), 245–49; A. Roulin, *Constant: Oeuvres* (Paris: Pléiade, 1957), pp. 1399–1411 and 1434–38. These various approaches are discussed with intelligence and fair-mindedness by P. Delbouille who adds his own conclusions in *Genèse, structure et destin d'Adolphe* (Paris: Les Belles Lettres, 1971), pp. 33–60. This latter work is a major piece of scholarship to which I gladly record my debt.
3. *On a très bien saisi le sens du roman. Il est vrai que ce n'est pas d'imagination que j'ai écrit.* Non ignara mali. *Cette lecture m'a prouvé que je ne pouvais rien faire de cet ouvrage en y mêlant une autre épisode de femme. (Le héros serait odieux). Ellénore cesserait d'intéresser, et si le héros contractait des devoirs envers une autre et ne les remplissait pas, sa faiblesse deviendrait odieuse (P,* p. 569).
4. See *P,* p. 1436.
5. See, for example, H. Guillemin, *Éclaircissements* (Paris: Gallimard, 1961), pp. 85–117. Also M. Levaillant, "Notes sur *Cécile* de Benjamin Constant," *Revue d'histoire littéraire de la France,* 52 (1952), 81–83.
6. See Andrew Oliver, *Benjamin Constant: écriture et conquête du moi* (Paris: Minard, 1970), pp. 149–64.
7. See Simone Balayé, "Mme de Staël et Mme de Malbée," *Europe,* 46 (1968), pp. 107–14.
8. *P,* p. 155.
9. See F. P. Bowman, "L'Épisode quiétiste dans *Cécile*," *Actes du Congrès Benjamin Constant (Lausanne, Octobre 1967),* Geneva; Droz, 1968, pp. 98–108.
10. See W. Pabst, "*Cécile* de Benjamin Constant, document autobiographique ou fiction littéraire?" *Actes du Congrès Benjamin Constant,* pp. 145–52.

11. *P*, p. 179.
12. *P*, p. 140.
13. *P*, p. 148.
14. *P*, p. 141.
15. *P*, p. 146.
16. See, for example, *P*, pp. 155 and 162
17. See *P*, p. 158.
18. *P*, pp. 174–75.
19. *P*, p. 180.
20. See *P*, p. 182.
21. *P*, p. 183.
22. W. W. Holdheim, *Benjamin Constant* (London: Bowes and Bowes, 1961), p. 40.
23. *P*, p. 17.
24. *P*, p. 8.
25. Professor Alison Fairlie has rightly and persuasively argued that "Ellénore is neither incoherently composite adjunct nor lifeless schematic abstraction." See her excellent article, "The Art of Constant's *Adolphe*: Creation of Character," *Forum for Modern Languages*, 2 (1966), 253–63.
26. See P. Delbouille, *op. cit.*, p. 120.
27. *P*, pp. 20–21.
28. See *P*, pp. 7–8.
29. *P*, p. 83.
30. *P*, p. 81.
31. See P. Delbouille, *op. cit.*, pp. 170–71.
32. *P*, p. 68. For further examples, and a detailed discussion of this aspect, see P. Delbouille, *op. cit.*, pp. 173–79.
33. *P*, p. 37.
34. M. Turnell, *The Novel in France* (London: Hamish Hamilton, 1950), pp. 114–17.
35. M. Turnell, *op. cit.*, p. 98.

Selected Bibliography

In view of the multiplicity of Constant's own writings, and of the studies devoted to his personality and work, the lists of primary and secondary sources given below are necessarily very selective.

More detailed bibliographies will be found in Talvart, H. and Place, J., *Bibliographie des auteurs modernes de langue française* (1801–1927), Vol. 3, 1931 and Cioranescu, A, *Bibliographie de la littérature française du dix-huitième siècle*, Vol. 1, 1969. These should be supplemented by Rudler, G, *Bibliographie critique des oeuvres de Benjamin Constant*, 1909 and Deguise, P, "État présent des études sur Benjamin Constant," *L'Information littéraire*, 10 (1958), 139–50.

The place of publication is Paris unless otherwise indicated.

PRIMARY SOURCES

There is no edition of Constant's complete works. However, there is an excellent selection, with notes, of some of his major writings in Roulin, Alfred, *Benjamin Constant: Oeuvres*. Gallimard (Bibliothèque de la Pléiade), 1964. This contains the full text of *Adolphe, Cécile, Le Cahier rouge*, the *Journaux intimes*, and several of the main political works. A number of pamphlets and speeches are also reprinted, together with selections from *Mélanges de littérature et de politique* and the two opening chapters of Book 1 of *De la religion*.

Other works by Constant which do not figure in this collection include:

Wallstein, tragédie en cinq actes et en vers, précédée de Quelques réflexions sur le théâtre allemand. Paschoud, 1809.

Collection complète des ouvrages publiés sur le gouvernement représentatif et la constitution actuelle de la France, formant une espèce de Cours de politique constitutionelle, par M. Benjamin de Constant. Plancher, 1818–19 (4 vols.).

Éloge de Sir Samuel Romilly. Béchet, 1819.

Mémoires sur les Cent-Jours. Béchet, 1820 (Pt. I), 1822 (Pt. II).

Commentaire sur l'ouvrage de Filangieri. Dufart, 1822 (Pt. I), 1824 (Pt. II).

Du Polythéisme romain, considéré dans ses rapports avec la philosophie grecque et la religion chrétienne. Ouvrage posthume de Benjamin Constant, précédé d'une introduction de M. J. Matter, Inspecteur Général de l'Université de France. Béchet, 1833 (2 vol.).

To these should be added the selection of political writings contained in Pozzo di Borgo, O, *Écrits et discours politiques par Benjamin Constant.* Pauvert, 1964 (2 vols.).

The main published collections of Constant's letters (by no means complete) are:

"Benjamin Constant et Madame de Charrière: lettres inédites," *Revue des deux mondes,* 6 (15 April 1844), 193–264.

Lettres de Benjamin Constant à Mme Récamier, avec introduction et épilogue par Mme Louise Colet. Dentu, 1864.

Lettres de Benjamin Constant à Mme Récamier 1807–1830, publiées par l'auteur des "Souvenirs de Mme Récamier" [Mme Lenormant], Calmann-Lévy, 1882.

Lettres de Benjamin Constant à sa famille 1775–1830, précédées d'une introduction d'après des lettres et des documents inédits, par J.-H. Menos. Savine, 1888.

"Lettres de Benjamin Constant à Mme de Charrière," *Revue de Paris,* 5 (1894), 673–718.

Journal intime de Benjamin Constant et lettres à sa famille et à ses amis, précédés d'une introduction par D. Melegari. Ollendorf, 1895.

"Lettres de Benjamin Constant à Prosper de Barante, 1805–1808," *Revue des deux mondes,* 34 (1906), 241–72, 528–67.

"Trois lettres inédites de Benjamin Constant" [to Mme de Krüdener], *Journal de Genève,* 9 March, 1908.

"Lettres de Benjamin Constant à Böttiger, 1804–1814, présentées par F. Baldensperger," *Revue politique et littéraire,* 9 (18 April 1908), 481–86.

"Lettere inedite di Benjamin Constant al Sismondi" [presented by C. Pellegrini], *Pegaso,* 4 (1932), 641–60.

L'Inconnue d'Adolphe. Correspondance de Benjamin Constant et d'Anna Lindsay, publiée par la baronne Constant de Rebecque. Plon, 1933.

"Benjamin Constant et Philippe Albert Stapfer" [letters published by Gustave Rudler] in *Mélanges Vianey.* Les Presses françaises, 1934.

Benjamin Constant et Mme de Staël. Lettres à un ami. Cent onze lettres inédites à Claude Hochet, publiées avec une introduction et des notes par J. Mistler. Neuchâtel: A la Baconnière, 1949.

Selected Bibliography

"Benjamin Constant et Mme Récamier" [14 letters presented by J. Mistler], *Revue des deux mondes* (1 September 1950).

Benjamin Constant: Lettres à Bernadotte, sources et origine de "L'Esprit de conquête et de l'usurpation," publiées par Bengt Hasselrot. Geneva: Droz, 1952.

Benjamin Constant et Rosalie Constant. Correspondance 1786–1830, publiée avec une introduction et des notes par Alfred et Suzanne Roulin. Gallimard, 1955.

"Douze lettres autographes de Benjamin Constant" [presented by H. Guillemin], *La Table ronde,* nos. 115–16 (1957), 7–28.

Levaillant, M. *Les Amours de Benjamin Constant, lettres et documents avec un opuscule inédit.* Hachette, 1958.

"Lettres inédites de Benjamin Constant" [published by D. Berthoud], *Revue de Paris* (October, 1964), pp. 65–75.

There are letters from Constant to Mme de Krüdener in Ley, Francis, *Bernardin de Saint-Pierre, Madame de Staël, Chateaubriand, Benjamin Constant et Madame de Krüdener.* Aubier, 1967; to Charles de Villers in Isler, M, *Briefe von Benjamin Constant, Görres, Goethe . . . und vielen Anderen. Auswahl aus dem Landschriftlichen Nachlasse des Charles de Villers.* Hamburg, 1879; to Victor Cousin in Barthélémy Saint-Hilaire, Jules, *M. Victor Cousin, sa vie et sa correspondance.* Alcan & Hachette, 1895 (3 vols). Vol. 2, 267–79.

SECONDARY SOURCES

Actes du Congrès Benjamin Constant (Lausanne, Octobre 1967), édités par Pierre Cordey et Jean-Luc Seylaz. Geneva: Droz, 1968. Important collection of papers by leading Constant scholars from several countries.

ALEXANDER, I.W. "La Morale 'ouverte' de Benjamin Constant" in *Studi in onore di Carlo Pellegrini.* Turin: Società Editrice Internazionale, 1963. Best study of Constant's views on perfectibility and progress.

ASSE, E. "Benjamin Constant et le Directoire," *Revue de la Révolution,* 15 (July, 1889), 337–56, and 16 (October, 1889), 105–25. Remains essential reading for this period of Constant's life.

BAELEN, JEAN. *Benjamin Constant et Napoleon.* Peyronnet, 1965. Informative in substance, if rather journalistic in manner.

BASTID, PAUL. *Benjamin Constant et sa doctrine.* A. Colin, 1966 (2 vols.). Enormous, detailed *summa* of Constant's ideas. Prosaic but essential.

BÉNICHOU, P. "La Genèse d'*Adolphe*," *Revue d'histoire littéraire de la France,* 54 (1954), 332–56. The growth of *Adolphe* from *épisode* to *roman.*

BENJAMIN CONSTANT

BERTHOUD, D. *La seconde Madame Benjamin Constant.* Lausanne: Payot, 1943. The main study of Charlotte von Hardenberg.
————. *Constance et grandeur de Benjamin Constant.* Lausanne: Payot, 1944. A sympathetic, perhaps overindulgent, portrait.
CAUVET, E. "Mémoire sur *Adolphe* de Benjamin Constant," *Revue des langues romanes,* 41 (1898), 204–38, 293–344. An early study which still impresses by the solidity and usefulness of the background information which it offers.
CORDIÉ, C. *Benjamin Constant.* Milan. Hoepli, 1946. Sound general work by this indefatigable student of Constant and of the Coppet circle.
COULMANN, J.-J. *Notice sur Benjamin Constant lue à la séance générale de la Société de la morale chrétienne.* Impr. Crapelet, n.d. (1831). Interesting portrait by friend and contemporary. Emphasizes Constant's love of liberty and feeling for equality.
DEGUISE, PIERRE. *Benjamin Constant méconnu: le livre de la religion (avec des documents inédits).* Geneva: Droz, 1966. One of the fundamental recent studies. Corrective and highly informative on Constant's philosophic and religious development prior to the publication of *De la religion.* Important bibliography.
DELBOUILLE, PAUL. *Genèse, structure et destin d' "Adolphe."* Société d'édition "Les Belles Lettres," 1971. Indispensible synthesis of recent scholarship as well as original contribution. Valuable bibliography.
DERRÉ, J.-R. *Lammennais, ses amis et le mouvement des idées à l'époque romantique, 1824–1834.* Klincksieck, 1962. Includes an excellent chapter on "Benjamin Constant, théoricien du sentiment religieux."
DES ESSARTS, E. "Les Théories littéraires de Benjamin Constant," *Revue bleue,* 6 (18 August 1906), 203–06. Somewhat disappointing but not negligible. Deals with an aspect that merits much more study.
DU BOS, CHARLES. *Grandeur et misère de Benjamin Constant.* Corrêa, 1946. Suggestive and sympathetic psychological study, overtaken at some points by the discoveries of more recent scholarship.
Europe, no. 467 (March, 1968). Over 150 pages containing a number of important articles on various aspects of Constant's life and work. Contributors include Balayé, Bowman, Courtney, Deguise, Fairlie, and Pellegrini.
FAIRLIE, ALISON. "The Art of Constant's *Adolphe:* Structure and Style," *French Studies,* 20 (1966), 226–42; "The Art of Constant's *Adolphe:* Creation of Character," *Forum for Modern Language Studies,* 2 (1966), 253–63; "The Art of Constant's *Adolphe:* the Stylization of Experience," *Modern Language Review,* 12 (1967),

[164]

Selected Bibliography

31–47. Three admirably perceptive articles by the leading English Constant scholar. Essential for the study of *Adolphe*.

GODET, P. *Madame de Charrière et ses amis d'après des documents inédits, 1740–1805*. Geneva: Jullien, 1906 (2 vols.). Vol. 1, 333–85, particularly relevant to the Constant/Mme de Charrière relationship.

GOUHIER, HENRI. *Benjamin Constant*. Desclée De Brouwer ("Les Ecrivains devant Dieu"), 1967. Excellent general study of Constant's religious ideas. Characteristic combination of careful scholarship and high intelligence.

GUILLEMIN, H. *Benjamin Constant muscadin 1795–1799*. Gallimard, 1958. Always vigorous, usually antagonistic, sometimes unreliable.

HOGUE, HELEN H.S. *Of Changes in Benjamin Constant's Books on Religions (with notes concerning an unpublished version of "Florestan ou le Siège de Soissons, poème" and other Works)*. Geneva: Droz, 1964. Essential for the study of Constant's religious evolution.

HOLDHEIM, WILLIAM W. *Benjamin Constant*. London: Bowes and Bowes, 1961. Brief, lucid, and intelligent general account of Constant.

JASINSKI, BEATRICE W. *L'Engagement de Benjamin Constant: amour et politique (1794–1796)*. Minard, 1971. Scholarly and discerning. Reprints some inaccessible texts in full. Corrects misconceptions concerning Constant's early relationship with Mme de Staël and analyzes his political beginnings.

MURRY, JOHN MIDDLETON. *The Conquest of Death*. London/New York: Peter Nevill, 1951. Part I is a translation of *Adolphe*. Part II is a very personal essay which sees Constant's novel both as "a meditation on the problem of love and death" and "a new revelation of the eternal truth of Christianity."

NICOLSON, HAROLD. *Benjamin Constant*. London: Constable, 1949. Lively and elegant general study though not always wholly reliable in detail.

OLIVER, A. *Benjamin Constant: écriture et conquête du moi*. Minard, 1970. A challenging personal reading of *Cécile* and *Adolphe*.

PELLEGRINI, CARLO. "Benjamin Constant dall'autobiografia al romanzo," *Rivista di letterature e moderne comparate*, 9 (1956), 165–290. Important synthesis of various earlier articles by this leading Italian scholar.

POULET, GEORGES. *Benjamin Constant par lui-même*. Seuil ("Écrivains de toujours"), 1968. Excellent study. Suggestive and well-documented interpretation of Constant's personality and ideas.

PUGH, ANTHONY R. "*Adolphe* et *Cécile*," *Revue d'histoire littéraire de la France,* 63 (1963), 415–23. An interesting, unorthodox contribution to the *Adolple/Cécile* debate.

RUDLER, GUSTAVE. *La Jeunesse de Benjamin Constant, 1767–1794.* A. Colin, 1909. The great pioneering biographical work which remains fundamental for Constant's early years and, particularly, his relationship with Mme de Charrière.

————. *"Adolphe" de Benjamin Constant.* Malfère ("Les grands événements littéraires"), 1935. Scholarly and literary-historical presentation of the novel. Overtaken at some points by later discoveries.

SÉVERY, W. and C. DE. *La Vie de société dans le pays de Vaud à la fin du XVIIIᵉ siècle.* Lausanne: Bridel, 1911–12 (2 vols). Vol. 1, esp. pp. 128–72 is very informative about the Constant family.

THOMPSON, PATRICE. *Deux Chapitres inédits de l'Esprit des Religions (1803–1804).* Geneva: Droz, 1970. New light on the evolution of Constant's religious ideas, their links with his politics, and the growth of *De la religion.*

TODOROV, T. "La Parole selon Constant," *Critique,* nos. 255–56 (August-September, 1968), 756–71. Revealing *nouvelle critique* type of approach to Constant's use of language. Overassertive at some points.

Index

Index